Anna Hanson Dorsey

Coaina : the rose of the Algonquins

Anna Hanson Dorsey

Coaina : the rose of the Algonquins

ISBN/EAN: 9783741191404

Manufactured in Europe, USA, Canada, Australia, Japa

Cover: Foto ©Andreas Hilbeck / pixelio.de

Manufactured and distributed by brebook publishing software (www.brebook.com)

Anna Hanson Dorsey

Coaina : the rose of the Algonquins

COAINA,

THE ROSE OF THE ALGONQUINS

INTRODUCTION.

We have no dislike to religious fictions; but where authentic facts are already too abundant for our limited space, we see no reason to lay aside realities in which divine grace has been the chief agent, and some human heart the real scene of the action, for the sake of suppositions or inventions of the mind, were they ever so pious and interesting.

When the following pages were presented to us by their well-known gifted authoress, we felt delighted with their beautiful diction and their deeply interesting incidents; still we would not have presented the rich sketch, had it been merely a fine tale. We therefore felt no ordinary gratification, when we received, a few days since, the reply which we subjoin, inclosing four pages of a closely-written letter from our venerable friend, Bishop de Charbonnel, containing, in substance, the whole history of Coaina. But let the illustrious authoress herself introduce, not the story, but the history of her admirable heroine:

WASHINGTON, January 27, 1866.

VERY REV. SIR:

After the time and labor I have expended on Coaina, I have it fully in my power to authenticate its truthfulness, under our

INTRODUCTION.

dear Monseigneur de Charbonnel's own hand. Some twenty five or six years ago, this saintly man, then a missionary priest in Canada, came to the Seminary of St. Sulpice, in Baltimore, for the purpose of learning the English language through a regular grammatical course of study. He was a nobleman of rank, and had long before relinquished his title and estates to a younger brother, in France, to become a missionary priest.

I learned this from my venerated old confessor, Father Delnol, who was Superior of St. Sulpice, and who introduced Father Charbonnel to us.

Father Charbonnel was in the habit of coming frequently to our house to converse in English with us, and we considered it a great privilege to entertain him at all times. One evening he brought the little manuscript which I inclose—his *first English composition*—which he read to us with all the pleasure and simplicity of a child, and to which we listened with the deepest interest.

Once launched on the subject of Coaina he gave us many interesting particulars of her history, not recorded in his little narrative. I was greatly interested, and promised him that I would at some future day elaborate and make it into a story. I have kept it religiously, partly on account of my promise, partly for the touching facts it relates, and partly as a relic of a saintly friend. Although Father Charbonnel was reticent on that point, I am *very sure* that he was the priest of the mission at the time these events occurred. He would not own to it, but allowed us to infer it. A year or so after he left Baltimore he was made Bishop of Toronto. In the course of a few years he resigned the mitre for the cowl.

In talking of Coaina he expatiated on Coaina's devotion to

the Blessed Virgin. Probably I have not been happy in bringing out this fact conspicuously, but no one can read the narrative attentively without feeling it. The names of the characters—except Coaina's—are fictitious, and so are some of the trivial incidents and embellishments.

The situation of the mission, the village, the calvary, the description of the people, the account of the "Taho," are all to be found in the "History of the Indian Missions in North America," which has been one of my favorite books for years past.

In writing Coaina, I had one special object in view, besides illustrating the beauty and triumph of religion, and that is to reprove the sins of uncharitableness, slander, and rash judgment, the three sins which crucified Christ. These are the sins of our age. I sometimes wonder, such is the prevalence of these evils among Christians, if true charity has become an obsolete virtue.

Would to God our clergy, and the Catholic press, would make a crusade against the specious, special, universal and—shall I say it—infernal sin of slander, in all its forms. I don't know that I ever found any thing more applicable to this point than the history of Coaina.

Sincerely and truly your friend,

ANNA H. DORSEY

COAINA:
THE ROSE OF THE ALGONQUINS.

CHAPTER I.

THE EVE OF THE ASSUMPTION.

NOT far from Montreal lies a beautiful lake, which is formed by the dancing waters of the Ottawa, and surrounded by picturesque hills, which slope in gentle undulations down to its sedgy margin. It is called Canaradago, or the "Lake of the Two Mountains." One of the hills is crowned by a Calvary, which is approached by a rugged, circuitous path, along the sides of which stand, at regular intervals, small rustic chapels, which are much visited by pious pilgrims, and where, during Lent, the congregations of the Mission devoutly perform the "Stations of the Cross," and sing, as they march in solemn procession towards the cross-crowned summit, the sorrows of Mary, the sonorous and mournful chaunt blending, in harmonious accord, with the penitential season, and the commemorative suggestions of the spot.

Straggling along the shores of the lake and up the slopes, partly hidden by the hills and partly sheltered by the dark primeval forest, which recedes gradually northward, and where the pines and hemlocks ever moan together the sad hymn of the centuries, nestle two Indian villages of a Catholic mission, which diverge to the right and left. The one on the right belongs to a remnant of the once powerful Algonquins; that on the left to a remnant of the Iroquois, who were, in former times, one of the great aboriginal nations of the north; but although such near neighbors, these two people are as distinct in manners and language as they were in the days of Carter and Champlain. These Catholic Indians are the descendants of the fierce savages who tortured the blessed Father Jogues, and martyred, with cruel and prolonged torments the noble and saintly Brebeuf. They live in lodges built of logs and covered with bark, and, during the spring and summer, cultivate their fields and garden patches, where they raise corn, squashes, potatoes, beans, melons and other useful vegetables and fruits; the women, sharing the lighter labors of the men, fish, dress skins and bark, dye the quills of the porcupine, spin and weave a coarse cloth, embroider the garments, leggings and moccasins, which they so ingeniously fashion, with beads, tinsel, porcupine quills and fringes; train their children in strict obedience to the rules of the mission, and in the autumn migrate, with their husbands and families, to the hunting grounds of the far northwest.

Devoutly christian as many of these Indians are, and deeming it their greatest earthly privilege to have a resident missionary priest among them to baptize and instruct their children and themselves in the way of salvation, to guide them aright while living and console them when dying, they adhere with tenacity to many of their traditionary habits and customs. On state occasions, they smoke the calumet as a sort of a ratification ceremony, wear proudly the trophies of the chase, cling to their nomadic habits, take a simple pleasure in gew-gaws, feathers, embroidered garments, and, at certain times, do not refrain from painting their faces with vermillion and other rich colors, and are ever ready to engage, with great zest, in their primitive and stirring games. Religion has stripped these children of the forest of none of their simple enjoyments or innocent customs. It has done more grandly, more divinely; it has transformed them from worshippers of idols to worshippers and adorers of the one true God—from a belief in a false and weird cosmogony, and crude mythological fables and traditions, to a firm belief and enduring faith in the wonderful story of the creation, of the birth of man, of the atonement of Jesus Christ and the divine establishment of His Church upon earth; made them children of that fold which acknowledges ONE LORD, ONE FAITH, ONE BAPTISM, and believes in the commandments of Almighty God, and the precepts of His Church. Thus, by an easy transition, it became a strange but devout pleasure to these primitive people, instead of offering sacrifice and libations to the great *Wendigoes* (giants,) to propitiate their favor whenever they engaged in any enterprise of hardship and peril, to invoke the protection of the Blessed Virgin, and ask the assistance of the prayers of the saints; to commend themselves, during their journey through trackless forests, and over rapid rivers, to the guardian care of the angels of God, instead of the elfish *Nee-ba-naw-baigs* (water spirits,) and the evil *Puk-Wedjies* (pigmies of the woods), to chaunt the plaintive *Miserere* and *De Profundis* as they bear their dead to the fur-lined grave, and implore of the Great

Spirit, for their souls, a "place of refreshment, light and peace," instead of performing the heathenish rites of old, which were practiced at the feast of the dead.

It was amongst this people, who are the fruits of the blossoming of the Canadian wilderness, whose rocky solitudes were moistened by the vivifying dews of the precious blood of Christ's martyrs, that the events which we are about to relate happened somewhere near the year 1838, and if our introduction has been somewhat prosy, it was necessary to a better understanding of the narrative, that it should be written ; therefore, patient reader, if you will accompany me to to the chapel of the Algonquin village, which stands on yonder knoll, under the broad shadow of the hemlock and sycamore trees which surround it, I will, without further preface, introduce you to Coaina, the " Rose of the Algonquins," and other personages of our narrative.

Something is in progress in and around the rustic chapel, into which the slanting rays of an August sun fall in trembling showers of gold through the quivering leaves, which indicates an approaching festival. Young Indian lads, with blossom-laden boughs from the forest, with trailing vines bedig'd with flowers of tropical hues, with baskets of mosses, with branches of wild roses, with great clusters of golden-rod, asters and the wood anemone, with wicker cages containing birds, with clusters of wild grapes, still clinging in purple richness to the graceful vines, and garlands of ground myrtle, glowing with thousands of coral berries, were grouped here and there around the chapel doors, talking in subdued but cheerful voices, their low converse interrupted now and then by a burst of innocent laughter, which sounded in sweet accord with the rustling of leaves overhead, the wild notes of the caged birds, the drowsy hum of bees, and the distant murmurs of the dancing waters of the lake. The lads peeped now and then into the chapel; they were waiting for some one who was within to come out and receive the floral treasures and offerings they had brought. Meanwhile they took pleasure in observing the beautiful and sacred objects and adornments of the altar, and the shrine of Our Blessed Lady of the forest.

"Look, Joseph," said a little fellow, standing beside a basket which was covered with burdock leaves, "Coaina has unrolled the banner, and is hanging it upon the wall behind the altar. Don't it shine? I've seen the sky look so often when the sun goes down."

"Ugh! that's a grand banner, 'Tony. That's the banner that the ladies of Montreal gave to the mission a long time ago. They worked it with their fingers, and it's full of real gold, pearls and rubies, and was blessed, at the cathedral, by the great chief of the Church, who wears a pointed crown," replied Joseph.

"What's all that upon it, and what does it mean?" asked little 'Tony; "Do you know Joseph?"

"Father Etienne took me into the chapel once, and unrolled the banner and explained it all to me, because I did not miss a single word in my whole catechism," replied Joseph, proudly. "I will tell you, but I don't know whether you'll understand it if I do."

"I'll try," said little 'Tony, humbly.

"Well, you see the eagle feathers, the bear and the arrows and things. That's the *totem*, (coat of arms,) of the three christian tribes. Under that, all in gold—red and yellow gold—with rubies done in so cunningly, are the three council fires, and over all, linked with the rest, you see, by devices of things most prized by our people, is what Father Etienne called the *Monogram* of Jesus Christ." Here both boys bowed their heads and made the sign of the Cross. "You see, 'Tony, that is all done with gold, and silver, and pearls; but what the word means I don't exactly know, and was ashamed to ask, but I thought maybe it was *His* Holy Name, in characters which I did not understand."

"Thank you, Joseph. Isn't it a great honor to have our totem on the banner with Christ's?" said little 'Tony, naively. "But look, Joseph, at that bright star upon our Blessed Lady's head!"

"Kaw! it is the sunshine!" said a lad standing by. Not irreverently, however, was this said. The boy was only constitutionally matter-of-fact, and could not make a star out of sunshine.

"Sunshine is the light of the Great Spirit, and it *does* look like a star. Anyhow, don't you wish it would stay there, for that's the way I think SHE looks in the land of the Great Spirit," said little 'Tony earnestly.

"Well, yes, I'd like that sunshine to stay there if it could, but it *can't*. I'd let it stay if I could, but *I* can't either, so it's no use to be wishing. I'd crown her with stars if I could reach high enough to place them, but as I'm not high enough, we"ll have to crown our 'white Mother,' (a name by which the Indians of the mission called *her*,) with flowers," said the matter-of-fact lad, moving off.

"See here, Joseph," whispered 'Tony, lifting up the burdock leaves that covered his basket, "will these do for the crown? I found them, under piles of leaves, down in the glen, near the dancing waters. Do you think Coaina will make a garland of them for Our Blessed Lady's head?"

"Oh, 'Tony, how beautiful! where did you find these white violets? I think they must have bloomed on purpose to crown our Mother on the Feast of the Assumption!" exclaimed, in clear, pleasant tones, the voice of a beautiful Indian maiden, who had just left off hanging festoons of flowers around the rustic railing which enclosed the altar, to come in search of fresh mosses for the shrine, and flowers to crown the Tabernacle.

"Oh, yes, Coaina! I think so, too," said little 'Tony, as he lifted his sparkling eyes to her face. "I found them down by the dancing waters, in the glen, under a great pile of leaves. My heart sings like a bird because you love them, Coaina."

"Yes, 'Tony, these are lovely!" said the maiden, lifting the rich, variegated mosses upon which the violets rested. "So like *her*," she murmured, "so fair, yet so lovely; so pure, yet so humble; so holy and modest, yet concealing all, and covering her divine honors with the poor garb of poverty and seclusion. Yes, 'Tony," said Coaina, aloud, "these look as if each one had dropped from a star—don't you remember the old legend I told you the other day?—and we will crown Our Blessed Lady with them."

As this is not a fiction which we are relating, having learned the facts we relate, some years ago, from Monsignor De C——, I will describe Coaina, who was not only known by her baptismal name, Coaina (Catharine), but was so beautiful, and so beloved for her great virtues and the sweetness of her disposition, that her people of the mission gave her the soubriquet of *To-hic*—The Rose. As Coaina stood, holding the moss and violets in her hands—the sunlight flickering down through the trembling foliage, sprinkling her from head to foot with glittering spots of gold—she was very beautiful. Her skin was like the pale, amber-colored satin; her forehead low and broad; her nose straight, with thin, expanded nostrils; her mouth, small and exquisitely formed, was rendered more beautiful by the white, even teeth, which the slightest smile revealed; her eyes, full of intelligence and spirit, were softened by long eyelashes, and crowned by brows so evenly arched and black that the old men used to laugh, and call her the "daughter of the two

bows;" the head was exquisitely poised on her
slender and graceful neck, and covered with a magnificent suit of glossy black hair, which she wore
simply parted, and gathered together in a massive
plait, which was coiled around, and fastened to the
back of her head with a silver arrow, a present
from a schoolmate, while she was at the convent
school of Notre Dame, in Montreal.

The crimson blood blushed softly in her cheek,
like the sun-tints in a ripe September peach, and
her lips were as ruddy as the holly berries that
glisten in coral richness amidst the snows of the
Canadian forests.

Yes, Coaina was very beautiful, and I am particular in describing her, because her young life
was so fully offered to Him who fashioned and
formed her wonderful loveliness, and modelled so
perfectly on the virtues of *her* whom, from all eternity, He had predestined to be the Mother of His
Divine Son.

Coaina was dressed according to the manner of
her people. She wore a short skirt of blue and
white striped woollen, and a soft doeskin jacket,
curiously embroidered with beads. Her moccasins
were also cunningly wrought in gay devices, and
her leggings of scarlet cloth were finished with a

gay little fringe of feathers at the seam. Yet over all there was such a charm of modesty that, had she been a veiled vestal, the influence of her purity could not have been more felt and acknowledged. Around her neck, suspended by a finely wrought silver chain—the gift of the good sisters of Notre Dame to their pupil—Coaina wore a medal of the Blessed Virgin and a crucifix, which she prized beyond all of her earthly possessions, and which, as she stood in the chapel door, glittered in the sunlight, as, moved by the pulses of her heart, they reposed on her bosom.

"There, Coaina, will these be enough?" cried a lad, throwing open a blanket containing thousands of pine blades, odorous with balms, which were to be spread over the chapel floor.

"Not quite enough," she replied. "Father Etienne likes the floor well covered, Piquet; you will run back to the pines for more."

"I *did* want to go to my rabbit snares to see how many rabbits I've caught," said the Indian lad; "all the rest got rabbits yesterday, and I got nothing but a musk-rat."

"Well, Piquet, if you care more for rabbits than you do for our Mother's festival, begone!" said Coaina, gravely. "We will get some one else to serve Father Etienne at Mass to-morrow."

"I *do* care for the rabbits, Coaina, but I won't give up the festival. Redpath's boy and two others have gone into the forest with their bows and arrows, and won't be back until night; but—but—" and the boy's dusky face flushed, "but I want to do something for our Mother!"

"That's brave, Piquet," said Coaina, laying her hand gently on the black elf locks of the boy's head. "You'll be a great hunter some day. The Great Spirit will bless you, because you have courage to do what is right. Run off now to the pines, and fetch me as many blades as the blanket will hold, and then, Piquet, the day after to-morrow you shall go with me into the forest to hunt." Just then she saw approaching the young chief Tar-ra-hee, the hereditary sachem of her people, and she turned swiftly and resumed her labors in the chapel.

"Winonah, will you fetch in the flowers and mosses which the lads have brought?" said Coaina to a young Indian girl who was busied about the shrine of our Blessed Lady. The girl came forward with an impatient air, and, although she bore a family resemblance to Coaina—being her cousin—no two persons could have been more unlike. Winonah's eyes were fierce and defiant, with a certain wild yet repellant beauty in them · her brow wanted the breadth and serenity of Coaina's, and her handsome mouth wore a proud and scornful expression. Her attire, without being immodest, displayed in its gaudy, flaunting style a vitiated fancy, and a vain, ambitious nature. Trinkets glittered in her ears, on her wrists, and around her slender ankles, while in her black hair she wore jauntily an eagle's feather, the *totem* of her father, who had been one of the great chiefs of their people.

"Why not fetch them yourself, Coaina?" she asked, sharply, "or make the boys bring in the baskets?" At this moment she caught sight of Tar-ra-hee, who lingered still about the chapel door, and suddenly smoothing the frown from her brow, she hastened forward, and, without seeming to observe his presence, began coquetishly to gather in the flowers.

"See, Coaina!" she said, "these asters and crimson berries will make such a lovely wreath for Our Lady."

"I think these will be more beautiful, because they are pure and white like her," said Coaina, gently, as she held up the white violets.

"No, they will not do at all," answered Winonah, to whose intense chagrin the young chief had moved away without noticing her; "I won't have them; the crown must be rich in color, and glow around her head like flames of red and gold. Oh, what a crown I will make!"

"'What is the dispute, my dear children?" inquired a voice which was gentle, but quick and firm in its tones. Both girls started, as, turning, they beheld Father Etienne, who had approached unseen, standing near them. Both knelt, asking his blessing—Coaina with head bowed, Winonah with eyes cast down, but with her head proudly erect.

"Now, my dear children," said the good priest of the mission, "what is the difficulty? Speak, Winonah, my child!" With a flushed cheek, Winonah told him frankly of the difference of opinion between herself and Coaina about the garland, without explaining, however, the secret cause of her jealous and angry interference, and showed him the flowers of her choice, and those of Coaina's.

"Make garlands of yours, my child, and festoon the mossy walls of our Blessed Lady's shrine, they will indeed look rich and brilliant there," said Father Etienne, gently; "but *these* must crown her—these fair and modest flowers, so symbolic of her pure holiness. Yes, Coaina, my child, you are right—make of them a rare garland, to crown and honor her on the Feast of her Assumption. So far, everything is beautifully arranged—ah—yes—the banner is just in the right place. "See, children, that the floor is well strewn with pine blades," added Father Etienne, looking around with an air of satisfaction, after which he walked away, blessing the children who were grouped around the chapel, who clung to his hands, and the skirts of his long *soutane*, as long as he would stay.

"Now," said Winonah, when he was well out of hearing, turning to her cousin with an angry countenance, "as you rule here, tell me what I am to do."

"Let us help each other, sister," said Coaina, gently.

"It was my wish to make the wreath for our Mother," said Winonah.

"You shall make it, Winonah. I was coming to ask you, because I have the tabernacle to dress, and so many other things to do."

"No; if I can't make a fine flaming wreath of the flowers that I like, I shall have nothing to do with it—you can make it yourself, and do the other things beside," replied Winonah, tossing her proud head.

"As you wish, my sister, only let us have the chapel ready for the morrow," said Coaina. "Come, children, bring in the flowers and mosses, and let us all work together." And with good will they all obeyed her directions, for she was the directress of the sanctuary, chosen by the vote of the congregation from among her young companions for the office, on account of her piety, docility, modesty and amiability.

But Winonah had no intention of leaving the decorations of the chapel entirely in the hands of Coaina, to hear on the morrow, from every lip: "Coaina made that!" "Coaina hung those garlands!" "Coaina, and none but she, could have made our chapel so beautiful!" "What would become of us without Coaina to decorate it for the festivals!" and a thousand other expressions of the like character. She had vented her angry spite on her cousin, and now she would, to please her own sinful vanity, take part in the preparations, and only do that portion of the work which was agreeable to herself. In a few moments she was busy twisting vines around the cedar pillars which supported the roof of the chapel; now she climbed lightly to the rafters, and hung the cross-beams with festoons of green, from which were suspended the scarlet trumpet-flower and wild grapes, until Solomon's Temple, with all its precious carvings, and traceries of fruit and flower, was not more beautiful. Still tripping along the rafters, with the agility and lightness of a bird, she added a cluster of golden-rod here, of the crimson-tinted sumack there, of white *immortelles* here, of wild roses there, weaving in the asters and other flowers with cunning skill among the green leaves and graceful tendrils of the vines, until her task was finished. "Oh, how beautiful! Winonah, how beautiful!" exclaimed Coaina, as turning from the tabernacle, whose decoration she had just completed, she looked up and saw the really charming effect produced by Winonah's taste.

"I am afraid," was Winonah's ungracious reply, "that Father Etienne will not like it, so long as you did not do it."

"Never fear that, my sister," answered Coaina, in the simplicity of her heart; "it is more beautiful than anything I could do."

As the sun declined toward the west, the arrangements for the morrow were nearly completed. The floor was strewn with blades of the odorous pine, every footstep that pressed them distilling a subtle aroma; the altar was a glowing mass of verdure and flowers. Our Lady's grotto had been lined with fresh mosses, a coronal of white violets encircled her brow, and a white lily, found among the sedges of the lake, was placed in her folded hands. The front of the grotto was draped and festooned with vines bearing rich hued flowers, among which, half hidden by the leaves, hung the wicker cages, containing birds, who uttered sweet wild notes of wonder, as they fluttered in their airy prisons, to be captives until to-morrow eve, when the festival would end—then, at the chapel door, amidst the laughter and happy converse of the children of the congregation, Coaina would unfasten the door of each cage and release them, giving them freedom, air, sunshine and their homes far off in the depths of the forest. This joyful little ceremony generally closed the festival days of the mission, and was particularly enjoyed by the young people of the congregation.

But the last glittering rays of the setting sun shoot between a gorge in the hills, and sparkle here and there like sacramental lamps—now upon the jeweled folds of the mission banner, now upon the gilded door of the tabernacle, now upon the burnished head of the crucified Christ, now creeping like a flame along the silver fringe of the altar cloth. A quiet and solemnity now reign where so short a time before was heard a busy hum. Here and there kneel groups of those who, having completed the preparations for the festival, now examine their consciences for confession. Coaina knelt close beside the shrine of the Blessed Lady, partly concealed by the flower-wreathed pillars near it. Amidst this devout silence, Father Etienne enters with the most Blessed Sacrament, which he deposits in the tabernacle, while every head is bowed low in adoration of that grand and mysterious Presence. He now takes his seat in the confessional, and soon is heard the low whisperings of penitent hearts, as one after another approach the tribunal. Dim shadows, thrown by the purple twilight, steal in at the open door, and with them come the old and young of the mission, walking silently and reverently, wrapped in their toga-like blankets; their dusky, grave faces, and long black hair, hanging loose about their shoulders, their noiseless motions and immobile features adding to the solemn effect and sacred repose of the consecrated place. The women knelt apart from the men, clustering around the shrine of the Blessed Virgin, their little children kneeling beside them, lisping their innocent prayers —all modestly attired, and all devout, save one, who, tall and shapely, and of a proud, haughty demeanor, knelt in a conspicuous place, where the trinkets in her ears, and the tinselled embroidery of her mantle sparkled brightly in the light of the sanctuary lamp, while her eyes, large and restless, roved critically and inquiringly around her, showing that her heart was but little in unison with the whispered prayers on her lips, as she slipped the beads of her rosary rapidly through her fingers. This was Altoninon, the mother of Winonah, and the aunt of Coaina, whom she had adopted in her orphaned infancy, and reared in her own lodge. Some one in a distant part of the chapel arises to approach the confessional, and when she sees that it is Tar-ra-hee, the young chief, she no longer looks around, but with an expression of satisfaction appears to recollect herself and attend more devoutly to her prayers. Thus it was within the mission chapel, but outside, wrapped in their blankets, stood two forms, their sharp, piercing black eyes scanning the scene within, while an expression of contempt and disgust pervaded their countenances. One was very old, and was named Ma-kee (Knife). He was by descent half Huron, half Algonquin, and had never been baptized, but lived peaceably among the christian Indians of the mission, some of whom were his near relations. The other was a dissolute, handsome and unbaptized young Iroquois chief, from the neighboring village, called Ahaeek (the Deer), who, having heard a rumor of the preparations, had come down to the Algonquin village to see what was going on, hoping that he should, by some chance, get a glimpse of Coaina, whose beauty and grace had made a profound impression upon him.

CHAPTER II.

COAINA.

THE Festival of the Assumption closed with the singing of the Litany of Loretto by the congregation, the sacred melody being led by the powerful and flute-like voice of Coaina. Swelled to a volume of rich sound, the holy chaunt floated out upon the calm evening air, its solemn echoes lost, in low reverberations, in the shadowy forest. Purple shadows, cast by the mountains, lay upon the lake and shore while the pines and firs along the ridges were fringed with the gold of sunset. Ere long, the inhabitants of the village assembled in a grove surrounding the great lodge, where the chief men were accustomed to hold council, and debate on any question which arose respecting the interests of their people. The chiefs and the old men, with Father Etienne in their midst, sat around the door of the lodge, placidly smoking, telling traditions of the old fierce wars with the Hurons and Mohawks, going over again the thrilling adventures of their great hunting expeditions to the northwest, or listening to Father Etienne's thrilling narratives of the early French missions in Canada. Old Ma-kee, over whose head the snows of nearly eighty winters had fallen, formed one of the group. Seated upon the grass near Father Etienne, wrapped in his blanket, with his chin upon his breast, he listened. He seldom spoke, for as he declared, "his breast was heavy at the degeneracy of his people, who had become women;" and when he did, it was to scoff at the new creed they had adopted, which he emphatically called the "smoke of foolishness." But the claws and fangs of the old lion were gone; he was harmless, and out of christian charity he was allowed a place of honor among his people, with a comfortable support, in the hope that, ere he died, his pagan darkness would pass away, and he, at least, receive the purifying sacrament of baptism. Ma-kee had great faith in, and respect for, Father Etienne, whom he knew to be a brave as well as a good man; but he did not hesitate to tell him, on occasions, that there was no reason or sense in what he taught, because no man could understand it. And in this the old pagan was no worse than the materialists of this, our day, who reject the mysteries of faith because their human reason cannot reduce them to its own level. Father Etienne was relating the marvellous escape of the French missionaries, nearly two centuries ago, and many of their catechumens, from the house of Saint Mary's, of Ganentaa, just when the Onondagoes had conspired with the Mohawks to massacre every soul of them. He described, with great spirit, the ingenuity and courage of the missionaries in effecting their escape, and the speechless amazement of their foes when they found the house so mysteriously abandoned. All listened with profoundest interest, the twinkling of keen black eyes and an occasional grunt of approval expressing their delight. When Father Etienne ceased speaking, old Ma-kee lifted up his head and spoke: "My grandmother," he said slowly, "remembered John Brebeuf. She was a Huron. When he was dying under the torture; when his fingers and thumbs were cut off; when he was pierced with lighted splinters, torn with scourges and hacked with hatchets, many of the prisoners around him, who had likewise been tortured all night, begged him for baptism. He had no water; none would give him a drop. The day dawned; at sunrise they were all to be put to death. The prisoners begged for baptism; there was not a drop of water. Brebeuf lifted his hands and eyes to the Great Spirit and prayed. Just then, my grandmother, very young at that time, came from the fields with her arms full of maize stalks. The long leaves and tassels were dripping with dew; it hung upon them like rain-drops. He saw it, and asked her for one of the stalks. He spake our language. She had helped to torture him, but she was a woman. She gave him two or three. He grasped them with joy; he bade the prisoners look up; he sprinkled them; he signed the cross in the air over their heads with the maize, and so they were baptized with the dews of heaven and his own blood. I think that was enough. But Brebeuf was a brave man. He died like a warrior; he should have been an Indian, ugh!" Having spoken, the dusky old pagan wrapped his blanket about him, and again dropped his head upon his breast, leaving his hearers variously affected by his simple and true narrative.

At some little distance from the great lodge, and nearer the lake, were the women, the young people and children of the village, standing or sitting in picturesque groups under the trees and along the shore. Some exercised themselves by running, dancing and leaping; others sought amusement in more quiet ways, while many played simple games with shells and plum-stones, peculiar to their customs. Blithely arose their cheerful voices in pleasant converse and innocent laughter, while each face wore a look of contentment and enjoyment. We said that every face wore a glad expression; that was a mistake, for Altontinon, who sat apart from the rest, gorgeously attired, as usual, looked dissatisfied; but no queen ever wore her royal robes more proudly than she wore her coronal of blue and scarlet feathers, her necklace and earrings of silver beads, and her embroidered scarlet moccasins and mantle. She was the widow of the deceased sachem of her people, and, in default of a son to inherit the dignity and title, had the mortification of seeing it pass to the son of her husband's brother, the present chief, Tar-ra-hee, whose baptismal name was Cyril. Bitterly disappointed, and obliged to bear, not only her own mortification, but that of her kinsmen, it became a grave consideration how to retrieve the loss. The idea suddenly presented itself to her scheming mind, one day, to marry her daughter, when of a proper age, to Tarra-hee. Once admitted, this idea became the ruling motive of her life; she was prepared to sacrifice everything to its accomplishment, and so pledged herself to her kinsmen, who gave it their hearty approval. Altontinon kept up a kind of state around herself, which no one cared to interfere with; for although she was a christian, she was not a saint; in fact, so far from being a saint, she was —I don't know whether there is a name in any Indian dialect for it—but, in plain English, she was a termagant. This woman had taken Coaina, who was left an orphan at a very early age, and nursed her at her breast with her own child, who was, to a day, of the same age. Strange to say, she had loved Coaina, and although she stormed at her now and then, and set her to drudgery that she spared Winonah, she was, upon the whole, kind to her. In the perilous journeys of the tribe to the distant hunting grounds, so full of hardships and privation, she cared as tenderly and constantly for the young Coaina as for Winonah, and ever took the same pains in teaching her those arts and accomplishments so necessary to the complete training of an Indian girl. Coaina was skilful and expert in them all. She excelled all of her young companions in domestic handicraft; she was more expert in dressing skins and dying quills and feathers; more skilful in fishing and hunting; more agile in running and climbing; more ingenious in embroidering and fashioning the garments, which she made with such celerity; and more quick in acquiring knowledge from the books she was permitted to read than any young person in the village. Her school tasks were never neglected; her religious duties never omitted, and as she grew towards womanhood, there was developed in her character so much purity, virtue and excellence, that she was not only the favorite of the village, but was constantly held up by parents to their children as a model for their imitation. She, unconscious of her superiority, was so modest and affectionate, so generous and cheerful that, with the exception of one, no heart felt malice, envy or ill-will towards her, and that heart was Altontinon's, who had noticed all this with ever-increasing discontent, and whose chagrin was now completed by the fact that Coaina had become far more beautiful than Winonah; that she was more intelligent and *more beloved.* Here was a cloud, and from it dropped the very gall and wormwood of bitterness into Altontinon's soul. Then arose the fear or presentiment that the superior attractions of her niece would frustrate all of her plans for her child's union with Tar-ra-heo. Henceforth her jealous misgivings gave her no peace, and on several occasions, when she fancied indications on the part of the young chief of admiration for Coaina, she became almost frenzied with rage. Coaina felt keenly the change in her aunt's conduct towards her, and although her unkindness cost the poor child many a bitter tear, she remained dutiful and patient, bearing all her humors with sweetness and in silence, and sought refuge and consolation only at the feet of MARY, towards whom she had ever cherished the most reverent and tender devotion, by whose life she had modelled her own, and whose gracious assistance she constantly implored. About this time Coaina was placed, by Father Etienne, at the head of the female confraternity of the Immaculate Heart of Mary, a position which Winonah expected and hoped to receive. This added fuel to the flame in the heart of the mother and daughter, who, by many a sneer, taunt and slight, aroused every indignant emotion in Coaina's nature, and rendered her life almost unendurable.

But as the storms and rains of March vivify and strengthen the roots of the forest trees, so did these tempests of ill-will and malice, which beat so perpetually and harshly against her, strengthen her soul, vivify her faith, and sweeten with eternal fragrance the sweet blossoms of humility that had such deep root in her soul. Then arose another cause of bitter envy and jealousy. On a certain occasion the two girls were permitted to go, with a party of their kinsmen, to Montreal to sell their bead-work and feathers. Father Etienne gave them a letter of introduction to the Superior of the Convent of Notre Dame, who not only received them kindly, but introduced them, at the hour of recreation, to the *religious* of the house, and also to the lady pensioners of the academy. The beauty of the two Indian maidens, the artless grace and modesty of Coaina, the proud mien and wildly bright eyes of Winonah, their excellent French, their low, sweet modulated voices and unsophisticated expressions, won upon every heart. The lady pensioners were half wild with admiration of these beautiful Algonquin princesses, and purchased everything in their baskets, besides making them presents of pictures and little ornaments in gold and precious stones, which they took from their own ears and fingers.

Not very long after this visit, Father Etienne received a letter from the lady superioress of this convent, in which she spoke of the visit of Coaina and her cousin, and after expressing the most friendly sentiments towards both, offered to receive Coaina at the academy as a pensioner for six months; at the expiration of which term, she would also receive Winonah for the same period. After due consultation with her friends and kinsmen, it was agreed that Coaina should accept the advantages offered by this kind invitation, and Father Etienne accompanied her, himself, to Montreal. Altontinon would have prevented it, had she dared, but she had made up her mind, that in all that she intended doing to carry out her plans, no agency of hers should be apparent; she was too proud, and prized the position she held too highly, to be willing to lose caste, so she gave a cold assent to Coaina's going, while she fumed in secret, and poisoned still more Winonah's mind against her innocent cousin. She told her, under a sacred promise of secrecy, all that she designed to do for her advantage, and found in the ambitious girl a willing ally.

Coaina was very happy in Montreal. Every one in the convent loved her, and took great pains in assisting her through her tasks. Quick and appreciative in everything they taught her, above all she showed such a passion for music, and so astonishingly was her talent developed by a little instruction, that she was regarded almost as a prodigy. Her voice was of such surpassing sweetness and compass, so full of a certain *wild life*, that ere long she was permitted to sing in the chapel choir, where, her heart overflowing with the love of Jesus and Mary, she sang the *Salve Regina*, with such sweetness and fervor that the notes soared and floated with thrilling effect above the grand thunder tones of the organ.

When the six months had expired, the good Sisters of Notre Dame would fain have detained her; they were unwilling to lose their beautiful favorite, but she desired to go, that she might take the place of Winonah in her aunt's lodge, and be to her indeed a daughter, in the place of her absent child. So she returned to the "Lake of the Two Mountains," and to her home, the same humble-minded, light-hearted, simple child as she left; and forgetful of the past, she remembered only the debt of gratitude she owed her benefactress, and determined to be more scrupulous than ever in the discharge of the duties she owed her. There was great joy in the village when she came back. Old and young had a pleasant greeting for her; Father Etienne gave her his blessing with his welcome; the children brought flowers and birds for her acceptance, and the old pagan Ma-kee lifted up his head and said: "The sunshine has come back to us, and the song of birds. It is good."

Winonah was kindly received at Notre Dame, but having no talent for music, and but little aptitude for study, the little she gained served but to increase her self-conceit and vanity; and at the expiration of her term, she was full of anger and ingratitude against the good *Religieuses*, because she had failed to learn what they found it impossible to teach her. This, so far from imputing to her own want of capacity, she charged to their indifference. This added fresh zest to the hatred of Altontinon for the innocent Coaina; but she dared not, as we said before, brave public opinion by open acts of violence to her; therefore, like the wily, malicious woman she was, she bided her time, and watched for her opportunity to give crushing effect to her revenge.

Thus matters stood in the village of the "Lake of the Two Mountains," up to the day on which our little narrative opens, and we are happy to say that no more digressions will occur, having put our patient readers in possession of all the necessary facts to enable them to comprehend as mournful a tragedy as was ever written, crowned by as saintly a martyrdom as the world ever knew.

Altontinon sat alone, still watching her daughter, who was sporting with other girls of her age on the margin of the lake, and wondering what had become of the young chief, Tar-ra-hee, whom she had not seen since Vespers. Her keen, restless eyes had been seeking him for the last half hour, but as yet he had not appeared, either among the chief men at the grand lodge, or with the young people on the shore. She became impatient, and was about to rise up from her seat, to walk round in search of him, when some one suddenly approached her, and asked, in a quick, impatient tone: "Altontinon, where is Coaina?"

She started round, and Tar-ra-hee, the young chief, stood before her.

"Is she not with her companions down there by the lake?" she asked.

"I will go and seek her!" he replied.

Now old Ma-kee, walking slowly, approached her and asked: "Where is Coaina?"

"Ask me where your grandmother's ghost is?" she said, sharply. "I do not know where she is."

"Altontinon, your rattles grow finely," replied the pagan, moving on.

"Where is Coaina, my child?" inquired Father Etienne. "I have not seen her since Vespers."

"I have not seen her for more than an hour, my father. Perhaps she is in the chapel," she replied, more respectfully. He went away. Group after group of young people approached, one after the other, all making the same, inquiry.

"We are waiting for her to begin blind man's buff," said one.

"We are waiting for her, to dance. Tar-ra-hee is asking for her," said another.

"We want her to sing for us?" said the children.

"We can't get along without Coaina!" cried one.

"Everybody wants her! where is she?" screamed another.

Almost beside herself with fury, Altontinon, who restrained herself with difficulty, professed to be entirely ignorant of the whereabouts of Coaina, and she was finally left alone, but not long; for presently little Tony straggled up and asked the so oft-repeated question : " Where is Coaina?" and received for answer a rousing slap, full on the side of his tawny cheek, which sent him roaring away. Soon after, Tar-ra-hee came back, his gay feathers nodding over his head, his silver ornaments, and a gold medal sent him by the English queen, glittering in the last glimmer of sunset—so full of life and courage, so graceful and noble in his bearing that, for an instant, Altontinon was lost in admiration ; but his words recalled her to her own train of thought, and again plunged her into the abyss of her own malicious intentions, for he asked if she had yet seen Coaina.

" I have not seen her ; can't the stars shine without Coaina ? can't the wind blow ?" she answered, in suppressed rage.

" No, the stars do not shine for me when Coaina is away," replied the young chief, with a proud nod." It grows always dark."

" Coaina no longer heeds me ; she is beginning to have lovers. Ahdeek, the Iroquois, has been around my lodge lately. Perhaps if you can find him, Coaina will not be far off," said Altontinon.

The young chief started and turned upon his heel, stung sharply, but too proud to question his tormentor. Altontinon thought, "he will now seek Winonah," and watched eagerly to see if he went towards her, but he strode off in quite another direction, and she lost sight of him.

Tar-ra-hee wandered listlessly and moodily on, heedless of whither he was going, when he suddenly halted and bent his head in a listening attitude; then a gleam of joy lit up his swarthy features. He was within a short distance of Altontinon's lodge, and had heard Coaina's voice singing, in low sweet tones, one of the hymns of the mission. He sprang forward, and swiftly made his way thither. It was, indeed, Coaina, seated at the door of the lodge, with the soft moonlight falling upon her upraised face. She heard advancing footsteps; the next moment Tar-ra-hee stood beside her. A deep blush crimsoned her cheeks; she arose and saluted him, with downcast eyes.

"I have come for you, Coaina. Your companions await you on the shores of the lake. Come!" he said.

"Did my aunt send for me?" she asked.

"No."

"I cannot come: do not wait."

"I will wait. You shall come!" he said quickly.

"Cyril!" exclaimed Coaina, who always called him by his christian name.

"Forgive me, Coaina; come!" he pleaded.

"No; I cannot go. You must return to them."

"I shall stay here," he said, in a determined tone.

"Don't—don't! you must go away!" she said, earnestly.

"I *must* go away!" he said, angrily. "Do you send others away? Why must I go?"

"Ah, Cyril, go, and do not be angry, my friend," she said, while big tears rolled over her cheeks. "I have something to do—a duty which I must not neglect—and should you stay away and be found here with me! ah, Cyril, don't you see how ill it would look?"

"Listen, Coaina," said the young chief, gravely; "I will obey you now, but give ear to my words, and open your heart to take them in. My lodge is empty, and before another moon I will rise up in the council, and ask for you to be my wife."

A soft blush suffused Coaina's lovely face, and a dreamy smile chased the tears from her eyes, but she only said : "Go, now, Cyril, my brother; leave me."

"I go, Coaina," but when the moon rises to the height of yonder red star," he said, pointing to one overhead, "you will hear my flute not far off from the lodge; will you listen to what it tells, Coaina?"

"I will listen, my brother," she promised. Then he turned, and moving swiftly away, was lost among the shadows of the night.

CHAPTER III.

THE SHADOWS OF THE STORM.

THE exultant gleam faded from Altontinon's eyes, for no sooner had Tar-ra-hee left her than she felt that her anger had got the better of her craft; and if she wished to succeed in her wicked designs, it was a most impolitic way to begin by offending him.

On that very day she had inaugurated her malicious work. She had positively forbidden Coaina to leave the lodge that evening, and had uttered a slander against her to Tar-ra-hee, by coupling her name with that of Ahdeek, the Iroquois, which she was crafty enough to know would, at some time or other, help to serve her purpose. She watched his retreating figure, satisfied that at least she had prevented him from seeing Coaina that evening; but when she saw, in the distance, that he turned into a lane of cedars which led to her own lodge, her baffled rage almost suffocated her. "He would see Coaina," she thought; "he will find out that her absence from the innocent enjoyments of the evening was compulsory, and having discovered this, would suspect *her*, and give no credit, henceforth, to anything she might assert to Coaina's injury."

The longer she sat there brooding over the failure of this, her first steps towards the accomplishment of her ambitious scheme, the more intense grew her hatred, and forgetting that All-Seeing Eye, before which the profoundest secrets of the soul are nakedly unveiled, forgetting all the divine teachings and claim of religion, forgetting death and the judgment, she vowed, with a bitter curse, that she would succeed in what she had undertaken, even if Coaina's reputation and life be the sacrifice.

But her guilty fears were somewhat lulled to rest when, later in the evening, she again saw Tar-ra-hee among the young folks, and observed that he showed much attention to Winonah, who exerted all of her coquettish wiles and arts to charm him.

The moon had arisen, full and unclouded, over the mountain, and everything glistened in her rays as if frosted with silver. The festival was over, and the people were returning to their peaceful homes.

Altontinon, well pleased at the notice bestowed upon her daughter by the young Algonquin chief, walked slowly homeward, full of thought concerning the advantages of a marriage between them. Winonah tripped along lightly over the dewy turf, a little in advance of her mother, whose eyes watched lovingly the gracefully moving form, whose every motion threw out sparkles and flashes from the spangles and gold fringes which adorned her tunic and moccasins. How she loved the girl, but how savage and pagan was the love which gave birth to sins which would incur the displeasure of God, and wound afresh the tender hearts of Jesus and Mary. It is said that when a soul voluntarily seeks *evil*, the prince of evil is ever ready with opportunities to serve its purpose, and so it seemed to be on this occasion.

Among the Iroquois who lived in the adjoining village, there were some few who, rejecting Christ, preserved their own heathenish traditions, clung to the ancient customs of their ancestors, and, it was whispered, practiced in secret their idolatrous rites. But as they were peaceable, and observed all the civic rules of the mission, and interfered in no way with their christian kinsmen or people, their presence was tolerated, in the pious hope that, after a season, they might be induced to follow their example. Among these was their hereditary chief, Ahdeek, (Reindeer,) who had often distinguished himself in their great hunting expeditions, and excelled in all those accomplishments most highly prized and appreciated by the Indians. Ahdeek was handsome, vain, passionate, and it was said that he was dissolute in his habits. He had frequently seen Coaina, and had, in various ways, endeavored to win a smile from her, by expressing his admiration by signs, gifts and words; but she had invariably repulsed every advance he had made, and turned from him with a frown of displeasure whenever he ventured to approach her; but all this only incited him to more persevering efforts to win her.

On the evening of the festival he had strolled down towards Altontinon's lodge, with scarcely a purpose except to be near the home of Coaina, for he supposed her to be absent at the festival, when, to his great joy, he saw her standing in the moonlight, leaning against the moss-covered stile that led to the lodge. She was reciting the rosary, her eyes fixed on the cloudless heavens, and thinking that, as the moon was throned in glittering beauty among the luminous stars, so was the Blessed Virgin throned in heaven, and surrounded by the glorious angels, whose queen she is. It was a consoling and beautiful thought, and as they twinkled and trembled in dewy splendor, flashing out rays of crimson, blue and gold, Coaina almost imagined that she saw the flutter of their glorious wings as they bowed before their queen.

"Left all alone, like a wild pigeon in the empty nest! I am glad to see you, Coaina," said the audacious Iroquois, who had approached her unseen and unheard.

"Ahdeek!" exclaimed Coaina, starting; "I wish you well, but you must go away this instant. I am all alone."

"That is good; now I can *say* to you, face to face, what you are blind and deaf to in signs. I love you."

"Esa! Esa! shame on you! Ahdeek, leave me!" she cried.

"I will become a christian, Coaina, if you will hear me!" he plead.

"To become a christian will be a glorious thing, Ahdeek! but go; Father Etienne will instruct and baptize you."

"No; I learn the christian creed from you or none. I thought you christians would give your life to save a soul."

"So would I lose mine to save your soul, Ahdeek, but I shall never enter your lodge; I can never be more to you than a friend. I will pray for you. You must now go away," and Coaina turned from him and swiftly entered the lodge, while he, baffled and angry, strode off, almost knocking Altontinon down, he came so suddenly against her. She, as keen-eyed as a vulture, had seen him, as she approached her lodge, talking with Coaina. At first she thought it was Tar-ra-hee standing at the stile, but when she discovered it was Ahdeek, the Iroquois, she said: "Aha! yes!" and rejoiced in her wicked heart, because she knew that his having been there would help her evil plans; then asking Ahdeek if "he kept his eyes in his pocket that he might run people down in his path," she went into her dwelling, and calling Coaina, assailed her with the most violent abuses; affecting to believe that she had received the Iroquois as her lover in her absence, she uttered the most injurious insinuations, nor would she listen to Coaina's explanations, but pretended to be outraged and grieved and horrified at her conduct, called her a hypocrite, and finally struck her in the face.

Almost stunned by the injustice and violence of her aunt's conduct, Coaina, without attempting to speak another word in her own defense, withdrew to her own little apartment, and dropping the curtain of skins which separated it from the rest of the lodge, she threw herself prostrate upon the floor before the blessed images of Jesus and Mary—of Jesus, in His bloody coronal of thorns—of Mary, of the seven dolors. She watered the floor with her tears; she offered her griefs to them, and finally found consolation in the generous resolve she made to suffer patiently all the unmerited reproaches she had received, for them who had suffered so willingly ten thousand more infinite and bitter griefs for her.

At last, her head resting upon her arm, she fell asleep, and was refreshed by the dreams of innocence. Once only did she awake. She had dreamed of her dead mother, as she sometimes did, and thought she was singing a soft lullaby to her, whose strange, unearthly melody thrilled through her heart, and awoke her. At first, she did not know whether she was awake or still dreaming, for she heard, while the whippowil sent his lamentations abroad through the forest, and the screech owl answered in shrill vibrations, the sweet wild notes of a flute, breathing assurances of a pure affection. Then she remembered Tar-ra-hee's promise, and while a soft glow stole over her tear-stained face, she commended herself to the protection of the Blessed Virgin and fell asleep.

Like a fair prairie blossom agitated by the morning winds, and scattering, in prodigal brightness, the dew-drops from its rich petals, so Coaina threw off the sense of ill which oppressed her when she first awoke. The first red beams of the newly-risen sun shone through the vines that partially shaded her window, and bathed in light the sacred images of Jesus and Mary, which stood upon a little shelf at the foot of her bed. "My Holy Mother and Advocate," she murmured, folding her long, tapering hands together as she knelt before them, "look at thy divine Son, and obtain for me a patience like unto thine."

Her simple toilet was soon made, and hurrying out to the chapel she knelt in her favorite place.

close beside the altar of the Blessed Lady, and assisted at Mass with the greatest devotion. Between the sweet and glorious mystery of the altar and the benign presence of Mary, Coaina's whole being reposed, as in a safe haven, secure from the rude storms that threatened her.

Tar-ra-hee served Father Etienne at the altar that morning, as he was frequently in the habit of doing, and it was a touching sight to see this noble young savage bowing in such sweet subjection to Christ; to see his strong arms folded in meek and childlike devotion; his proud, handsome head bowed, in unquestioning faith, before the Lord of lords, whom he received humbly and reverently under the form of Bread.

For several days nothing occurred to interrupt the tranquillity of the Village of the Lake. Altontinon behaved to Coaina with a certain grave displeasure, and when she addressed her, spoke in a tone so harsh and sneering that she was deeply pained; but feeling innocent of offense and guiltless of crime, she omitted none of her duties, and persevered in all her accustomed attentions to her aunt and cousin, hoping, by patience to overcome evil, and by prayer to turn their hearts forgivingly towards her. She observed that Altontinon had many and long secret conferences with several of her kinsmen and friends, and was surprised, once or twice, to see her in close conversation with Ah-deek, the Iroquois.

Tar-ra-hee had not approached her since the night of the Festival of the Assumption; she only heard his flute, now and then, under the trees around the lodge, and except that Father Etienne and her friends around the village greeted her as kind as ever, and the little children gathered about her and hung upon her skirts whenever she appeared among them, she would have indeed felt friendless.

The clouds were gathering around her, and their shadows were discerned by her delicate and sensitive perceptions; she knew not whence they were coming, or in what storms they would burst; she trembled with the chill that often swept over her; she felt that no mortal could help her in this mysterious coming woe; but the darker grew her dread, the closer she clung to the shelter of the sanctuary, the oftener she fortified her soul with the divine sacraments, and with more constant fervor did she kneel at the feet of Mary, imploring her gracious protection.

But one day the clouds seemed suddenly to disperse, and again streamed the sunshine into Coaina's heart. Father Etienne walked into Altontinon's lodge while herself and daughter were partaking of their evening meal, and Coaina, who was no longer permitted to eat at the same board with them, sat apart, busily engaged upon a piece of needle-work. Each one arose to welcome him; he returned their salutations with a cheerful air, and taking the chair placed for him, he drew it to the side of Coaina, and sat down. Altontinon's guilty heart was agitated by this unexpected visit; but when the good priest announced the object of it, she felt as if a bolt of ice had suddenly fallen upon it. "I have not only brought you my blessing to-day, my good children," he said, "but also most excellent tidings. This morning, while the assembly were in council, deliberating about the sale of some lands on the St. Lawrence, which they finally decided not to sell, Tar-ra-hee stood up and declared his intention to make our child here, Coaina, his wife, and asked the consent and approval of all present, including myself. There was not a single voice raised in dissent against it; in fact, there was a murmur of satisfaction very audible, for we all knew, Altontinon, how precious is To-hic to her people. They are all proud of their 'rose,' and each one felt that the young chief's choice of a bride was not only a wise one, but a special pleasure to each individual present. When I was called upon for an opinion—sit still, Coaina—I not only hastily approved of Tar-ra-hee's choice, but assured him, before all present, that in such a union he would find all the good and happiness that, humanly speaking, one could expect; after which," continued Father Etienne, laying his hand gently upon Coaina's bowed head, "the assembly ratified its solemn approval and formal consent, and I hurried here to be the first to bring the joyful news to your aunt, and give my blessing to the betrothed of the good and brave Tar-ra-hee."

"Thank you, my father, for your goodness," she said gently, and without lifting her modestly downcast eyes; "Cyril is generous, but it is best, my father, not to hope for too much. I have sometimes seen," she said, lifting her great soft eyes, and looking before her with a strange, far-off expression, "the day which rose the brightest close in wild, wintry tempests."

"Coaina, my child, these are dreams. It is the christian's duty to receive with joy and gratitude whatever good our Father sends, without throwing a veil of cloud and doubt over His gifts," said Father Etienne, cheerfully; but many and many a time since has he remembered her looks and words that day.

"I will try, my father, to be grateful—to be dutiful; but there's something," she said, passing her hand over her forehead and eyes, "there's something like a mist—I don't know what it is, but it seems to shut out the sunshine."

"Coaina," said the good father, "if you were a pale-face, I should say you have the *vapors*. You have been keeping in-doors too much of late, and stooping too long at a time over this everlasting bead work and stitching. Altontinon, see to it, or we shall have a burial instead of a bridal."

"I will see to it, my Father," replied Altontinon, with a double meaning; then dissembling with a self-possession worthy of a better cause, she rallied Coaina while she congratulated her, and pretended to be highly delighted at the alliance. "Leave her with me, my father," she continued, "she is only coy—you know how modest Coaina is—she has to think a little while—where a girl has two or three lovers, it is difficult to decide all at once——"

"My father," said Coaina, in response to Father Etienne's look of inquiry, "I have no lover—that is, I shall be the wife of Cyril, or none. He is all that I could ask or desire." Coaina knew that her aunt meant mischief by this hint, and that she referred to Ahdeek, the Iroquois; she therefore answered as she did, with a slight hesitation, because she remembered that Ahdeek had presumed to call himself her lover; and such was the tender and sacred regard which this young Algonquin maid had for the truth, that she would not fully deny her aunt's statement, lest she should thereby offend the truth.

"Well, well, my child, cheer up! You have a happy future ahead. Altontinon, hurry the wedding preparations, for I am sure Tar-ra-hee will not desire a very long delay," and Father Etienne, giving but little thought *then* to what had passed during the interview, hurried up to the Iroquois village to one or two sick persons who needed his ministrations.

The news flew through both villages, in an incredibly short time, that Tar-ra-hee had chosen the Rose of the Algonquins for his bride. Coaina received the hearty congratulations of old and young, of friend and foe, until she, to escape their friendly jests, and the incessantly repeated good wishes of those who constantly crowded to see her, generally slipped away from them, and by a back path found her way to the chapel, to offer her newly-found happiness to the Blessed Virgin, and hide her modest blushes in the shadow of the sanctuary. We spoke of Coaina's "friends and foes." It is marvellous that so pure and lovely a nature should have a foe; but alas! it is a world old story how virtue ever excites malice; beauty, envy; prosperity, covetousness; and felicity, hatred and ill-will; so, after all, it is not strange that our Rose of the Algonquins had her enemies who, to conceal their plans for her ruin, assumed the guise of friendship, and were loud in their protestations of delight at her good fortune.

Never was happiness and prosperity borne with greater modesty. The cloud that had shadowed her heart seemed to have passed away. Altontinon and her cousin were more kind, and the strong, protecting love of her betrothed, gave her a feeling of tranquil happiness. No duty was left neglected; no kindness left undone; no pleasure or assistance that she could afford was withheld. Skilled, as we said before, in hunting and fishing, she brought the choicest dainties of the lake and forest to her aunt' lodge, and so deftly did she perform all her tasks, so important had she become to Altontinon's comfort and Winonah's whims, that her aunt began to

feel what a terrible loss Coaina would be to her
This was another incentive to her to carry out her
selfish and malicious plots against the guileless
maid, for whose approaching marriage the most
splendid preparations known to these primitive
people were in progress.

CHAPTER IV.

"BEWARE OF THE SNAKE, TO-HIC."

IT is well for the reader of this narrative to keep
this fact in view: that had the young chief of the
Algonquins united himself in marriage with Winonah, it would have increased the dignity and consequence of her mother's family, as it would have
secured to them the chieftainship and grand *totem*
of the tribe. Bitterly disappointed in their ambitions and selfish aspirations, angry and disturbed
in mind, they were prepared to unite with Altontinon in any plan she might suggest to them to
break off a marriage so disastrous to their schemes
of arrogance and pride. It seems strange to associate the vices of civilization with the characters of

an Indian story; but believe me, friends, that human nature, unless wonderfully dignified and hallowed by grace, is the same latent savage everywhere, which only requires circumstances, in a greater or less degree, to rouse him from his lair in the heart to seek his greed or revenge. Let us not, then, be too much surprised, however much we may feel grieved at the depravity of these disappointed people, or deem incredible the events which follow. It was not long before whispers began to float about to the injury of Coaina, which at first only excited a scornful expression of denial from her friends. She, all unsuspicious of the plots against her happiness, was as blithe as a bird, wondering often, in her sweet humility, why she should be so blessed! Her eyes, like a young doe's, grew softer and more luminous, and her voice, ever trilling in sweet cadences, like the wild birds of the forest, became more low and gentle, and was only heard when her full heart sought to give expression to her grateful happiness, singing the beautiful litanies and touching hymns of the mission.

Not the least rejoiced of all her friends was old Ma-kee, the unbaptized, who would sit watching her—often in her aunt's lodge; sometimes on the shore; sometimes at the door of the chapel, while she adorned the shrine of the Lady with flowers—his withered face wearing a grave and pleased expression, and only breaking the silence to take his pipe from his mouth, and say: "Ugh! it is good!" The affection of this old pagan for Coaina, I have sometimes thought, in connection with her sad story, was a grace bestowed upon him for that act of charity showed by his grandmother to the martyr Brebeuf!

Of those most enraged at Coaina's approaching marriage, was Ahdeek, the Iroquois, who found a ready sympathizer in Altontinon, and readily enlisted in the service to aid in the accomplishment of that which would finally throw Coaina, helpless and defenceless, in his power. He was now frequently seen at Altontinon's lodge. This was not agreeable to Tar-ra-hee, who, without suspecting any designs against his betrothed, nevertheless so despised the low vices of Ahdeek, that he could not bear to know the air she breathed was contaminated with his presence, and desired her to hold no intercourse with him, but leave the lodge whenever he came into it, which she invariably did.

Day after day rolled on, and the month of the falling leaves had come. The frosts had tinted the leaves with the most gorgeous hues of crimson and orange, which, blending with green and russet, and relieved by the rich evergreens of cedar, pine and hemlock, gave to the forests the appearance of a grand *parterre*. Nature seemed to be preparing her robes for a grand festival, instead of a burial. There is something sublime in this glorious passing away of summer, as if in thus gathering about her departure a splendor symbolic of a glad obedience to the law of the great Creator, she offers a holocaust of precious adoration, and crowned with a silvery nimbus, expires like a blood-stained martyr, full of the joyful hope of a resurrection to come. Taking their lessons from the dying year, it is not strange that the Indians, in the primitive days, should have chanted their death-song, when life was passing, their eyes fixed in hope on the setting sun, whose radiance, they believed, illuminated the pathway to the hunting grounds of the Great Spirit.

The Indians of the mission of the Lake of the Two Mountains, were preparing for two great events—one was the marriage of their chief, which Father Etienne desired should be celebrated with great solemnity, not only to impress upon his people the dignity of the sacrament, but to offer to Tar-ra-hee and Coaina a tribute of respect, which he considered them eminently worthy of; the other was the annual migration of the tribe to the hunting grounds of the Northwest.

The young ladies of Montreal, who had known and loved Coaina at the Convent of Notre Dame, sent her a magnificent bridal present of a dress of blue velvet, made in the style of the picturesque attire she wore when they first saw her, embroidered with silver, and a veil of blue crape covered with spangles. They knew her singular devotion to the Blessed Virgin, and thought, justly, that the present would be more acceptable if composed of *her* colors. In the same box, neatly packed, and directed to their beloved pupil, was a wreath—made by the nuns, with the permission and approval of their superior—composed of delicately tinted feather flowers, among which were woven clusters of Roman pearls. Directed to Father Etienne's care, he no sooner opened the box than he sent for Coaina, to whom he presented them with genuine pleasure.

"My father," said Coaina, looking upon the costly presents spread out before her, "these are very rich and beautiful! They are too fine for me. I should be ashamed to wear them. I have prepared a more simple and befitting attire."

"Coaina, my child, these things must be worn, according to the intention which prompted the gifts. You cannot refuse to do so without appearing proud and ungrateful, which you *are not*. If I thought they would give birth in your heart to one single throb of vanity, I should at once advise you to burn them up. But wear them, my child—it will please your good friends in Montreal; it will please Tar-ra-hee and your people to see you splendidly dressed on your wedding day. After that, you can wear them for penance, if you choose," said Father Etienne, laughing. "Now take them home, my child."

"Yes, my father; but something has happened—I am troubled—may I speak to you?" said Coaina.

"Yes—yes. But, my child, what is the meaning of all this? I confess that you perplex me!" said Father Etienne, perceiving, as he looked up, that Coaina's eyes were full of tears. "What is the trouble?"

"There is something, I do not understand *what*," she said, timidly, "that causes some, who were formerly my best friends, to curl their lips at me as they pass; they have no greeting for me when I salute them, but look me full in the face, and, with a toss of the head, turn away."

"Tut! tut! my good child! I fear that it is a little envy on *their* part, and a little imagination on *yours*. Did you never hear, Coaina, that when one is about to marry, all one's faults are trumped up and magnified, and when one dies, all of one's virtues are only remembered. So don't give yourself unnecessary trouble about one's looks. Looks can't hurt one. So that your conscience is clear, and each duty performed with a view to the approval of Almighty God, why should you be disturbed? Go home, my child, assured that *she* who is the 'Help of Christians' will be your refuge and protection."

"That is my hope!" she replied, with a smile that irradiated her countenance—"that is my hope!" Then, kneeling, she received Father Etienne's blessing, and went away loaded with the rich gifts which she was to wear at a supreme moment, but not as a bride. She had never hinted to Father Etienne anything relative to the unkind treatment which she had for a long time received from her aunt and Winonah, because she not only feared to wound charity thereby, but believed, in her humility, that all she suffered was due to her unworthiness; nor had she ever referred to her annoyances about Ahdeek to him, not caring to trouble him about trifles ; and in fact, although the effect of these annoyances was so disagreeable and serious a matter to her, there was scarcely anything tangible or grave enough in them to justify an appeal to Father Etienne ; he was, therefore, at that time, entirely ignorant of all the undercurrent of deceit and wickedness that was going on, to the prejudice of Coaina. Altontinon and Winonah approached the sacraments regularly. Alas ! yes ; they dared to approach the august feast of the altar, as Judas did ; they dared invite Jesus Christ into their hearts, which were the abode of devils ; they dared again to crucify Him by their malice towards His faithful servant, who, in return, prayed for them night and day, and frequently offered her worthy communions for their temporal and spiritual good.

One evening, Coaina, having remained later than usual in the chapel, where she had received much consolation in prayer, returned home, and found her aunt and Winonah in raptures over a superb mantle of mole-skins, fringed richly with gold, and lined with cloth. Coaina had never seen anything which struck her as being so magnifi-cent, in her life, and she expressed her admiration with simple earnestness, without once inquiring to whom it belonged. If she thought about it at all, her idea was that it belonged to her aunt. What, then, was her surprise when Altontinon threw it over her shoulders, saying: "Tar-ra-hee knows how to make princely gifts to his bride. The Queen of England might be proud of this."

"Oh, how I wish I were you, Coaina!" exclaimed Winonah, clasping her hands.

"For me! Oh, it is too grand, too costly for me! When was Tar-ra-hee here?"

"This afternoon, while you were at the chapel. He will not be back until to-morrow evening. He has gone, in his canoe, to fish, up the Ottawa, and the word he left is that you meet him on the shore when he returns, with his gift, this superb mantle, about you," said Altontinon.

"How foolish is Tar-ra-hee to have me make a show of myself," she said, with a low laugh, as she smoothed the velvety fur with her small dusky hand. "I shall, however, do as he wishes; really I am ashamed of such grand finery."

"It is not too fine for the bride of our sachem, Coaina! Why, gold, and silver, and precious stones, would not be too grand for *you!* But what have you got there?" said Winonah.

"Something which I will show you by and by," replied Coaina, who had felt Winonah's sneer, and then, gathering up the mole-skin mantle with the other things which she held in her arms, she retired to her own apartment. Then Altontinon and Winonah embraced each other, laughed and danced as if they were wild, and making other signs expressive of triumph, pointed towards Coaina's apartment with fiendish glee.

The next evening Coaina folded the mole-skin mantle and hung it upon her arm, then threw a gray cloak about her in such a manner as to conceal its gold fringes and scarlet lining, and was about leaving the lodge to go down to the lake to wait for Tar-ra-hee, when her aunt accosted her with a discomposed look.

"Where are you going, Coaina?"

"To wait for Cyril, as he left word," she mildly answered.

"Oh! But where is the mantle? He was very particular in his wish for you to wear it," said her aunt, anxiously.

"I have it here," replied the unsuspecting girl, as she lifted her cloak, that Altontinon might see it. "I could not wear it through the village without exciting too much observation, so I thought I would put it about me after I got down to the lake."

"Such modesty!" said Altontinon, scornfully. "Little hypocrite, leave off that gray cloak this instant, and wear Tar-ra-hee's gift, as he bade you. He shall not be dishonored by having his wishes, as well as his bridal present, slighed in that way. Shame upon you." Then Altontinon snatched the grey cloak from Coaina's shoulders, shook out the superb mole-skin mantle, and before Coaina, in her surprise, could offer the slightest resistance, she had put it around her, and fastened the showy gilt clasps over her bosom. "Now go," she added, "you are too poor-spirited to be the wife of our chief."

What was it that, like a strain of clear music, suddenly whispered to Coaina's heart: "*Blessed are the poor in spirit, for theirs is the kingdom of heaven?*" She could not tell, but, repeating the words to herself, she walked from the lodge, forgetful of all else, while her eyes wore that same far-off expression which we have before described. She did not see the scornful looks directed towards her, or the low-uttered sneers as she passed the various groups collected in front of the lodges in the village, on her way to the lake; still less would she have understood them even had she seen them.

The soft music of the waves rushing swiftly to the shore, and melting upon the sands—the cool, crisp wind, and the broad track of gold and crimson light thrown across the lake by the declining sun, roused Coaina from her far-off dreams, or rather from her introverted communings; and, selecting a sheltered seat upon the gnarled roots of an ancient maple, whose branches, laden with scarlet leaves, leaned down and partially swept the surface of the lake, she folded her hands upon her knees, and awaited the coming of Tar-ra-hee. At length, afar off, and in the very midst of the sun's golden track, his canoe appeared upon the dancing waters; nearer and nearer it sped like an arrow, under the sinewy strength of the young chief's arms. Coaina could now see the paddles flashing in and out of the water, looking as if they were plated with burnished gold; then they were drawn in, and Tar-ra-hee stood up, his symmetrical form showing in noble relief against the bright sky; his eye swept the shore; Coaina waved a bright scarf with which she had covered her head; he made a glad gesture with his hands, again resumed his seat, and by a few vigorous strokes of the paddles brought his birchen canoe gliding swiftly up upon the sands. Securing some of the finest and largest of his fish, he sprang upon the shore and hastened towards Coaina, who, with a smile of welcome, modestly advanced to meet him, when he suddenly halted— his face flushed crimson, and an angry scowl darkened his features.

"Cyril!" said Coaina, timidly.

"Thou art fine to-day, Coaina, too fine for the bride of an Algonquin christian," he said, scanning her for a moment with grave scorn, from head to foot, then passed on with quick, angry step. Here was sudden darkness for Coaina! His own gift, worn at his own command to show her value for it, to excite such cruel anger! It was a mystery which was inexplicable to her. Tears gathered in her eyes, her hands trembled, and she was obliged to sit down while she tried to unclasp the mantle. Bewildered and grieved, she returned slowly homeward, the mantle hanging upon her arm, and when she was once more within the solitude of her own little apartment, she tossed it into an obscure corner, and, with a feeling of desolation, knelt, weeping and sorrowful, to lay her griefs where she had ever offered her joys, at the feet of Jesus and Mary.

By and by she grew more composed, and began to hope for the best. Guileless herself, she suspected no evil in others—far less did she imagine the existence of any base designs against her. After a while Altontinon came in under pretence of borrowing a needle, and asked: "Did Tar-ra-hee come?"

"Yes, he came," replied Coaina.

"Were you there in time to see him?"

"I saw him."

"How did he think his bride looked in that royal mantle?" asked Altontinon, with an evil glitter in her eyes.

"I believe he thought it, after all, too fine," she said, looking down.

"The unreasonable! But, child, it was no use to cry about *that*. Tar-ra-hee is only like all other men—none are constant," said Altontinon, with a sneer.

"I think that Cyril is. Nothing can shake my faith in him. We must not judge him rashly," said Coaina, gravely.

"I won't dispute the point with you. Settle it yourself. But did you hear that there's great sickness among the Iroquois?"

"No. Poor people! What is it?"

"A sort of dreadful fever. Father Etienne has

gone up there to baptize some of them who are dying. It is worse up near the forest, where the unbaptized ones live."

"Ah, may God bring them safely into His fold before their departure!" exclaimed Coaina, forgetful of her own sorrow, as she thought of the needs of the dying.

"And," continued Altontinon, "that filthy pagan, Ahdeek, has been here blubbering like a woman, and looking like a scare-crow, because his mother is ill and won't let the medicine man come in to her. Then he told me to ask you to talk to the WHITE MOTHER for her."

"I will, most gladly," said Coaina, who was only too happy to be engaged in a work of charity. Then she bathed her face, and wrapping her gray cloak about her once more, started to go down to the chapel to pray for the sick, and particularly implore the assistance of the Blessed Virgin for the conversion of Ahdeek's dying mother. Near the chapel she met old Ma-kee, who stopped her to inquire where Tar-ra-hee was.

"At his lodge, I suppose, Ma-kee. He has just returned from fishing."

"He is not there, To-hic. He started an hour ago for Montreal," said the old Indian. "Ugh!

Black clouds open their wings in the face of the sun sometimes. It is nothing strange—but beware of the snake, To-hic; beware of the deadly moccasin creeping in the grass!" Then Ma-kee wrapped his dirty blanket about him, and crept on.

"What is this shadow that comes darkening my heart?" thought Coaina. "I thought it was gone forever, but I feel the chill of it again. O, Great Spirit," she cried, prostrating herself before the altar, "Thou sendest us joy; Thou sendest us sorrow; whatever Thou doest is right; only keep me by the hand while the danger passes; let me cling closer to thee, sweet Mother of Jesus, that I may not perish in the dark waters!"

Two or three days passed by, and Coaina saw but too plainly that her people looked askance at her. Some refused to notice her at all—others returned only a haughty nod to her salutations, and once, when she met Father Etienne, she imagined that, although he spoke kindly, he received her with a stern and troubled expression of countenance, neither stopping, as usual, to say a pleasant word, or lay his hand upon her head in blessing. Even the little children began to shrink from her, and stood back, gazing wonder-eye'd at her, whenever she addressed them, or sought to gather them about her. She felt bewildered by the strangeness of it all, but Father Etienne had told her that perhaps "it was half envy on the part of others, and half imagination in herself"—therefore it might be so ; she would not resent it, but bear it patiently, in the good hope that GOD would accept her humiliation, which she offered in the true spirit of penance, in satisfaction for the many faults of her life, and in His own good time disperse the cloud which gathered so loweringly over her. Altontinon and Winonah were jubilant, and affected to be extremely kind to her, while Coaina, nothing doubting their sincerity, received their extraordinary attentions with gratitude, and felt comforted that they at least clung to her.

CHAPTER V.

LURED INTO THE SNARE.

EVERYTHING wore a change for Coaina—everything except the consolations afforded her by the divine sacraments. There was no change there. Untainted by the world, for whose salvation they were established, neither time, malice nor all the powers of hell combined can shake them from their eternal foundations, or strip them of the least of their attributes. Not of the "earth, earthy," they never fail those who are faithful to them, and though all mankind stand against the soul, they, with infinite generosity, undying compassion, unselfish constancy, and prodigal love, encompass it round about, never ceasing their consoling ministrations, until that soul has reached the end of its thorny pilgrimage, and passed the portals of death to its everlasting reward.

Coaina realized the truth of this in a wonderful degree, for the more her "kinsmen and friends stood aloof," the more constantly did she seek rest for her wounded spirit in the life-giving sacraments, and shelter her troubled mind in the shadow of the sanctuary. She could understand nothing except that a time of tribulation had come upon her; she could do nothing save put her trust in the justice and mercy of God, and the tender compassion of MARY, and patiently await the result.

One day after confession, Father Etienne asked her "if she had ever received any gifts from Ahdeek, the Iroquois?"

"Never, my father."

"Do you often see Ahdeek, Coaina?"

"Sometimes, at my aunt's lodge."

"Nowhere else?"

"Never, my father. Why should I?" Ahdeek is nothing to me."

"Very well; I do not see why I should doubt your word, Coaina."

"Thank you, my father," she replied gently. "My tongue never lies."

"Be careful, my child, that it never does," said Father Etienne. Then after a pause, he added: "There are evil reports abroad concerning you, Coaina; I doubt them all, and shall continue to do so until their truth is proved. If false, you are reviled without cause, and God Himself will succor you; if true, then, my poor child, you are guilty of the most detestable hypocrisy. Being only man, I cannot read your soul, and in the absence of proof of your guilt or innocence, I dare not withhold the sacraments from you. The responsibility rests, then, upon your own soul. Go in peace."

She would have spoken, but a sob choked her utterance, and rising from her knees she hastily left the confessional, and fell, rather than bowed, at the feet of the image of the Immaculate Mother. She could not fashion the anguished emotions of her soul into words; she felt, like her divine Saviour, all the bitterness without the guilt of the things whereof she was accused, and of which she was yet ignorant. Low sobs expressed her bitter suffering, and every tear she shed was an eloquent appeal to the compassion of God, as she knelt there, the innocent victim of the malice of her enemies.

No prayer ever uttered by prophet or saint can compare with the adoration of a speechless woe, which resigns itself in dumb resignation to the Divine will. His face may be hidden for a while by the cloud which veils it, but He is ever near; and when His designs are accomplished, He disperses, by a single breath, the shadows which hid Him, and lifts up the fainting soul with tender consolations, ofttimes crowning her with glory and eternal honor.

Where was Tar-ra-hee? He had returned from Montreal, and remained at home a week. One evening Coaina, after decorating the shrine of the Blessed Virgin with a garland of rich flowers which she had that day gathered in the forest, knelt down to recite the Rosary. While she dropped bead after bead, she thought of the sorrows that had crowned and pierced the immaculate heart of MARY, feeling all the time the sting of her own strange grief, until tears gathered in her eyes and rolled over her flushed cheeks. A quick, soft step entered the chapel, and then some one knelt, unperceived by her, not far from her. Covering her face with her hands, she bowed her head, resting it on the feet of the pure image of the Virgin Mother, and murmured: "Thou wilt not forsake me, my Protectress and Mother. Be thou my friend and consolatrix; then if all the world forsake me, what need I fear?" Her devotions over, she was about leaving the shrine, when some one touched her lightly upon the shoulder, and a familiar voice uttered her name in a low tone. She turned quickly, recognizing the voice, and saw Tar-ra-hee regarding her with a grave and sad expression of countenance. A crimson blush mantled her face; she stood suddenly still, while her tearful eyes rested with a wild and startled expression on his face. He walked to the side door of the chapel, where thick vines drooped over a sort of trellised work, forming a vestibule screened with leaves and flowers, and beckoned her to him.

"I am glad to see you, Cyril," she said, standing before him with her hands folded, and her eyes modestly cast down.

"Is that what you also say to Ahdeek?" he asked, gravely.

"Who, Cyril? The Iroquois? I am never glad to see *him*."

"But you receive his gifts, Coaina!"

"I have never received aught from Ahdeek," she said quickly.

"And never see him—and never go to the forest to meet him?" exclaimed Tar-ra-hee.

"Never, Cyril. What could have poisoned your heart to believe such a dreadful thing?"

"Coaina, I thought, a few moments ago, when I saw you kneeling there so humbly, your head bowed like a magnolia flower after the storm, that you must be innocent, or you dared not pray. My heart melted like the ice in the Ottawa, when the warm spring tides break it up, and I only thought of my love for my betrothed. But Coaina, what you say is not white; it is a lie."

"Oh, Cyril—Cyril, my brother!" she cried, in anguish; "tell me what you mean! What have I done?"

Then he told her about the mole-skin mantle. Ahdeek had shown it to him months ago, and told him it was to be worn only by his promised wife, and for that he was reserving it. He told her how unworthy Ahdeek was, and how blighting to a virtuous reputation was all association with him. Then he told her how his joy had suddenly turned into anger and mourning the day he returned home from fishing, and found her waiting on the shore for him arrayed in Ahdeek's gift.

"And was it not *your* gift, Cyril? My aunt——" then a divine charity closed her lips.

"Did any one tell you it was from me, Coaina?"

"I thought so, Cyril; it was left for me. I thought it was *your* gift, and I wore it that evening to show you how much I valued it," she said earnestly, while the truth declared itself in every line of her now pale face.

"Is this true, Coaina?" he asked, sternly.

"Our Blessed Mother is my witness that it is!" she replied, making a gesture with her hand towards the shrine. "Cyril, fearing the Great Spirit whose eye sees all, I dare not lie to thee, my betrothed.'

"Poison has touched my heart," he said, looking down into the innocent and truthful face uplifted to his. "To-morrow, Coaina, I will see you again in the presence of your aunt, and if any have calumniated you, they shall answer to me for it." And as he spoke, the troubled and gloomy expression of Tar-ra-hee's eyes gave place to one more gentle and tender.

"Thank you, my brother," she replied, and was about to leave him when Altontinon bustled into the rustic vestibule, outside of which she had stood, and not only watched them through the leaves, but overheard all that passed, and said to Coaina in an agitated tone:

"Hasten home, Coaina; my child is ill. I fear the Iroquois fever is upon her. I am going to Makee's lodge for herbs."

"I will go, aunt; I hope Winonah is not ill of the fever," she answered gently, while a dawning smile once more gave serenity to her features.

"Yes, *go!*" thought this malicious woman; "it

is all over for you, although you seem to think the sun is rising once more." Tar-ra-hee had re-entered the chapel, and was kneeling before the altar during this short conference; and when Coaina, after a rapid walk, reached home, she found Winonah apparently ill of a burning fever, moaning and tossing on her pillow, as if in the greatest pain. Had Coaina but turned down the coverlid, she would have seen that Winonah was surrounded by heated bricks, which almost consumed her, and produced all the effects of violent fever. But so innocent and guileless was this saintly child of the forest, that she never suspected any one of deceit or wrong; indeed, so full was her heart of a divine charity, that she only thought of concealing the faults of others, even when she discovered them.

The most criminal of all lies are those which are garnished here and there with the truth, making a plausible array of facts which can scarcely be contradicted without making the truth suffer, by dragging it through the mire of misrepresentation and falsehood, into which malice has plunged it. Never suspecting the practical lie before her, Coaina, in the simplicity of her heart, set about making her cousin comfortable. She gathered balm leaves from the garden and made her a refreshing drink, and bathed her head with cool water from the spring; she bound plantain leaves about her wrists and darkened the lodge, after which she arrayed everything neatly, and spread the table for the serving meal. In her happiest moods she always liked flowers about her, and now that her interview with Tar-ra-hee gave her a promise of returning tranquillity, she gathered a rich cluster from the aster and chryssanthomun bushes, which cluster around the doors and windows of the lodge, and set them in the midst of the table. It was quite twilight by the time she completed her arrangements. Winonah seemed to be sleeping, and Coaina went to the door to await the return of her aunt, when a lad—she could not distinguish his features—sprang over the stile and handed her a folded scrap of paper, then ran off again with the greatest speed. It was so dark that she could not distinguish a word of the writing which she perceived was in it, so hurrying in, she stirred the embers, and cast into the glowing coals a knot of resinous pine, which quickly kindled, and threw out a ruddy blaze which illuminated every part of the room. Then opening the letter, she read:

"My child, come to me directly, to the hut just beyond the pines, outside the Iroquois village.

Two young girls are dying, and will be baptized if you will come to them. Hasten. FATHER ETIENNE."

Without waiting a moment to consider, Coaina stepped in to see if her cousin still slept, and finding that she did, she wrapped her cloak about her and went forth, as she thought, on an errand of charity, at the bidding of her spiritual guide; but instead of that she was lured away, like a young gazelle, into the snare of the hunter, to suffer the crowning effort of the malice of her enemies.

That night also, Tar-ra-hee received a mysterious notification "to keep watch from day-dawn until sunrise," from a cliff which was overhung by an uprooted hemlock tree, that projected over the road leading to the Iroquois village, and commanded a view of two or three miles extent. He was told "to expect something which would unravel a mystery, and open his eyes to the truth." Troubled in heart, and full of but one thought, he determined to go, hoping that the unravelled mystery would be the full exculpation of Coaina.

CHAPTER VI.

THE IROQUOIS LODGE.

Coaina had no difficulty in finding the lodge designated in the letter. She paused a moment to rest, having walked very rapidly, then lifted the curtain of deer skins which hung over the entrance, and walked in; but she found no one there except an old woman, who feebly smoked her dirty pipe as she crouched in a corner upon a bed of bear skins.

"Where is Father Etienne?" asked Coaina, gently.

But the old squaw was deaf, and only stared at her with her bleared eyes. By and by a lad came in, who, when he saw Coaina, started to run out, but she caught him by the arm, and asked: "Where is Father Etienne?"

"He says you must wait. He will come presently."

"It is good," she answered. "But who is ill?"

"Hush—sh—sh!" said the old squaw, seeing that they talked, and pointing towards the inner recesses of the lodge, which were curtained off with skins.

"Are they very ill?" she asked the lad.

"Ugh!" replied the lad, shortly and sullenly, for he had glanced at the old squaw in time to see her shaking her shrivelled fist towards him—a warning which he knew from experience was not to be despised; then he slunk out of the lodge. Coaina, thinking only of the object which led her there, and nothing doubting but that Father Etienne would come presently, took out her rosary, and, holding it beneath her mantle, began the decade of the five sorrowful mysteries; offering her intention for the dying *ones* she had come to assist. She drew back into an angle formed by the irregular wall of the lodge, and partially concealed by a bark-covered cedar post which helped to support the roof, she closed her eyes, and was soon lost to all her strange surroundings in her devout meditations upon the august dolors of Mary. The sound of muffled footsteps, and that soft, indescribable rustle of garments, roused her attention, and thinking that Father Etienne had come, she unclosed her eyes, but saw, instead of Father Etienne, a crowd of dusky forms, whose hideously painted faces and gaudy attire, whose keen, cunning eyes and gleaming hatchets, filled her with perplexity and alarm. Among them, in the centre of the group, she recognized Ahdeek. According to the ways of her people, Coaina seldom showed either surprise or alarm, and now she calmly arose, and stepping forward, asked once more: "Where is Father Etienne?"

"He is not here, To-hic. This is a strange place to seek him," he replied.

"He sent for me here. Here is his letter," said Coaina, as a cold sensation thrilled through her heart. Ahdeek took the letter, while a gleam of triumph shot across his swarthy visage, pretended to read it, then tore it into pieces, and scattered the fragments with a scornful laugh.

"So," said a leering old chief, "the Algonquin christian can come to the lodge of the Iroquois medicine man, to see Taho. What will the man of prayer say?"

"I came here to see two Iroquois maidens baptized into the christian faith. Where are they? I will go to them," she replied, with an undaunted look, as she attempted to pass the group of Indians, for the purpose of leaving the lodge. But instantly a score of bright hatchets and knotty clubs were lifted over her head. Startled and terrified, but outwardly calm and brave, she folded her hands upon her breast, and looking full into the grim faces which scowled around her, she asked, in a clear and distinct tone: "By what right do you hold me prisoner?"

"By *my* will!" said Ahdeek, and every one of his dusky satellites responded "Ugh!" "You have curled the lip in scorn of the chief of the Iroquois," Ahdeek went on to say; "he is strong, and not to be driven off like a dog!"

"Have I ever harmed you, Ahdeek? It is not the part of a brave chief to make war against a defenceless woman. Let me go free," said Coaina.

"Listen, Coaina. My lodge is empty. I have no one there to light the fire upon my hearth; no one to dress the skins that I take in hunting, or cook my fish and venison. I need you. Be my wife. You shall have all that the daughter and wife of a great chief needs. You shall not toil. You shall have the softest furs of the stone-marten and fitch; your robes shall be decked with sables which I will fetch from the dark Suaganay; and your couch shall be spread with the soft skins of the beaver. You shall have the brightest beads, fringes of gold and silver, stuffs with all the colors of the rainbow, and plenty all the year round. Will you come to my lodge, Coaina?" said Ahdeek, hoping to dazzle her by his boastful promises.

"No, Ahdeek. No. I am already, in the sight of heaven, the spouse of Tar-ra-hee, the chief of the Algonquins. Even were I not, I would not come into the lodge of an unbeliever," replied Coaina, still standing bravely erect.

"The chief of the Algonquins would rather marry my old grandmother there than you, Coaina. The eagle will never mate with the carrion-crow. Tar-ra-hee despises you. What will he say when he knows where you spent the night?" asked Ahdeek, with a malicious grin.

"Ah, Ahdeek," wailed Coaina, as a full sense of her peril broke upon her mind, while she stretched out her hands towards him, "be generous, and let me go hence in peace."

"You are my captive until the day dawns. You shall have a new baptism, Coaina, then I will conduct you safely home. You are safe, To-hic, unless you do yourself hurt; only be quiet in the trap into which you are snared," he said. He then gave a brief order to the savages around to guard the entrance to the lodge, while two kept watch on each side of Coaina, watching her faintest movement. There was no hope of escape, for this swarthy crowd was composed of those among the Iroquois who still rejected christianity; who believed in the traditionary fables of their people, the superstitious rites associated with their worship; who had unlimited faith in the evil spirits of the water and forest, in magic and omens; who worshipped corn as a deity, and adored fire; who were unscrupulous in their morals, and believed in no higher law than obedience to their chief, and a due observance of their traditionary customs.

"Ahdeek," she said, in a solemn and impressive tone, "Ahdeek, you have betrayed me. You have snared me like a simple cony of the forest; but remember that my God is powerful—that He will bring to nought your wickedness, and make you fall into the pit you have dug for me."

"Let Him help you now, To-hic," said Ahdeek, scornfully. "Now's the time!"

"In His own good time will He deliver me. I adore His will, and await His coming," she said, clasping her hands together, and looking upwards with a gaze so supernaturally bright that one would have thought her sight penetrated far beyond the night, and beheld the face of the great Deliverer of whom she spoke.

"She talks of the great Manito," they whispered

around her. "She has the heart of a warrior."

Coaina saw how futile were her hopes of escape, and, with a sharp human pang, she resigned herself to the bitter necessity of her situation, while she implored the protection of Almighty God, and invoked the assistance of the Immaculate Mother. She felt that, beside these, she had none else to fly to. She knew that on the morrow she would be scorned and cast out by her people, for who would believe in her innocence, in the face of such evidence, when her reputation was already tainted by calumny? Her enemies had snared her, and thrown over her innocence a garment of blackness which no eye could penetrate save the sleepless eye of the All-seeing; which no glance of loving compassion could fathom save *hers*—the Mother of Jesus; which all would shrink from with scorn, save the angels who were given charge over her. In one sense we may exclaim: "Poor, forlorn Coaina !" In another we may exclaim: "O, maiden of divine predilection! honored art thou in thy sorrow and shame! thy thorny griefs are budding heavenly blossoms for the crown which is weaving for thee in heaven!"

Thus resting in strong faith upon God's promises, Coaina's troubled heart grew more calm. The rich blood had forsaken her face, leaving it cold and pale, and as she stood leaning against the cedar post, she looked like a statue carved out of stone, so motionless and apparently breathless was she.

Suddenly a bright red gleam shot across her closed eyes. When she opened them she saw a pyramid of faggots heaped up in the middle of the lodge, under which a fire had been kindled, and now shot here and there, between the interstices of the wood, red tongues of flame, which crept in and out like fiery serpents. Around this fire stood, first in order, the children and young people, and behind them, those more advanced in life. In the centre was the medicine man, in his grotesque trappings, and hideously disguised.

At a signal from him, all raised their hands; he threw a piece of deer's fat into the flames, when every one present cried out, in a measured and unearthly chant: "Taho! Taho!" After this, a small space was cleared by the medicine man, who now produced a pouch in which there was a pipe and powder, which he called *potu!* The pouch was carried solemnly around the fire, all chanting Taho! Taho! after which the *potu* was taken from the pouch, and distributed to all the men, who smoked it, and fumigated their bodies with it as with something sacred. An Iroquois filled a pipe with it, and lighting it by his own, handed it to Coaina, who, by a quick movement of her hand, dashed it to the ground and placed her foot upon it, exclaiming: "In the name of Christ, I trample on all idolatry!"

This enraged the Indians beyond expression, and they would immediately have done her violence for her contempt of a right which they held sacred, had not Ahdeek interposed his authority, which they, on the present occasion, sullenly obeyed.

At length the dawn crept through the crevices of the lodge, and ere long a deeper glow of crimson heralded the rising of the sun; then Ahdeek approached Coaina, and told her she was free to go. She sprang from the lodge, like a wild doe from the trap of the hunter, hoping to escape the attendance of Ahdeek, with which he had threatened her, and get back in time to be present at Mass; but he, watchful of every movement, was in an instant by her side, and—well named the Deer—easily kept pace with her swift footsteps. Glorious was the rising of the red and golden light out of darkness; brilliantly fell the splendid rays upon the hoar-frost, which glimmered like myriads of tiny crystals on the grass and leaves; joyfully dashed the scarlet-crested woodpecker from tree to tree; a low warbling echoed fitfully and sweetly among the gorgeous foliage of the forest; and here and there, chattering over their forage, the grey squirrels, with feathery tail erect, scampered up and down the branches. Nature smiled, rejoicing over the birth of this new day, which was so full of sorrow to the young Indian maiden, now hastening homeward, all heedless of the brightness around her, and compelled to bear the presence of her enemy, who kept close behind her, determined not to separate himself from her until the eyes of all the village had witnessed her shame. Suddenly an object standing on the edge of a projecting rock, and half hidden by an overhanging hemlock tree, arrested Coaina's attention; she shaded her eyes with her hand, and looked intently for an instant, then, uttering a low cry, she stretched her arms towards it, but it disappeared in the shadow of the forest, flitting away like a mist before her eyes. Then she fell fainting to the ground. It was Tar-ra-hee!

Altontinon had sought him the evening before, and told him, with protestations of reluctance, and had even shed tears, that the Iroquois held that night the festival of Taho; that she had good reason fcr knowing that certain of their people would be present, and advised him, as chief of his tribe, to watch and see if any baptized Algonquin attended it secretly—then she hinted at her hidden griefs about Coaina, darkly intimating things which she declared she dared not disclose. This interview following so close upon the mysterious billet he had received, aroused in Tar-ra-hee's mind the most suspicious vigilance. He could not sleep, but long before dawn took his station upon the overhanging rock we have described, and there waiting patiently, with a dull, heavy misgiving at his heart, he at last saw Coaina emerge from the Iroquois lodge, attended by Ahdeek. It needed no more to convince him that Coaina was not only false to him, but that she had lived a most hypocritical life, and was unworthy of a regret. He was a christian—he would not, therefore, revenge himself upon the Iroquois by taking his life; he would formally and publicly annul his betrothal to Coaina, and, leaving her to the punishment her crime deserved, go away from the tribe, to hunt along the shores of the dark Sauganay.

This was the conclusion which, after long and silent cogitations, he arrived at; then he sought Father Etienne, and laid bare his heart before him;

after which he privately consulted with the chief men of his people, and notified them to meet in solemn assembly the next day.

Pause an instant, reader, whether young or old, and reflect on the evils of malice, slander and rash judgment. We have seen how innocent Coaina was, how truly pious and unblemished was her life before heaven ; and yet we behold her clothed with depravity as with a garment, a despised and rejected outcast; wearing all the appearance of guilt and hypocrisy, through the *pride, malice, ambition* and *envy* of others, who, still esteemed and honored, triumphed for a season in their wickedness. *And remember, friend, this is no fiction !* Coaina actually lived and suffered as our feeble pen describes, and to this day the young girls of "the Lake of the Two Mountains" will lead the stranger to her grave, and with fast-falling tears relate, as they twine wild flowers around her place of rest. her mournful story.

CHAPTER VII.

LIKE A SHEEP BEFORE HER SHEARERS, SHE WAS DUMB.

WHEN Coaina saw Tar-ra-hee watching from the crag, and knew that he must have seen her leave the Iroquois lodge followed by Ahdeek, she felt as if some one had given her a heavy blow on her head; she staggered and grew faint and dizzy; then everything like brightness faded out of the air, and she fell to the earth, bereft of consciousness. Ahdeek stood, for a moment, perplexed and irresolute, but an idea suddenly presented itself which not only solved the difficulty of his position, but turned the accident to account; so, lifting the light and insensible form of Coaina in his strong arms, he sped swiftly to the village of the Algonquins, passing each wondering group he met without speaking, until he reached the lodge of Altontinon, who met him at the door with her hair dishevelled and her face disfigured with weeping, surrounded by three or four of her relatives, who all pressed silently but eagerly forward to look upon the pallid face lying so helplessly upon the shoulder of the Iroquois.

She had alarmed the whole village, the night before, by reporting Coaina's disappearance, professing all the time, the greatest grief and uneasiness about her, even while she secretly exulted in the certainty that she had fallen into the snare spread for her by her malicious arts. Now, when she saw Coaina brought to her door dead, as she thought, her pretended grief was changed to genuine alarm, and wringing her hands, she uttered the mournful and peculiar cry called by the Indians *wakonowen*, prolonging its shrill cadences until the whole air echoed with its sad notes, and one after another, within range of its sound, hurried hither, until quite a crowd had collected in and around the lodge.

"She is not dead," said Ahdeek, laying his light burden down upon a pile of skins and furs hastily thrown together by Winonah and some of the women. "She is not dead," he continued, as Altontinon paused in her lamentations to take breath, while every ear was strained to catch all that he had to say, "but the *Taho* was too much for her."

"The *Taho!*" screamed a woman, drawing her two little girls close to her. "Was Coaina—the child of our Blessed Mother—the Rose of our tribe *there!*"

"Esa! esa! and she the head of the Confraternity of the Rosary!" exclaimed another.

"And to think *we* were always taught to try and be like *her*," added a young girl.

"*I* almost felt afraid to touch the hem of her garment!" said Winonah.

"Oh, the detestable hypocrite!" said an old squaw, wagging her head.

"To think how we all loved her!" said a young girl, sadly.

"Think of her deceiving Father Etienne and our young chief! It is good she was caught in time!" said a grave looking woman, who had not yet spoken.

Old Ma-kee now edged his way feebly through the crowd, and stood looking down on the still, piteous face of Coaina. The muscles in his old withered cheeks worked, and a wonderfully tender and sorrowful look came over the usual fierce expression of his eyes. He stooped down and smoothed her small dusky hand, and laid his own shrunken, tawny hand lightly upon her forehead. Then he stood up and said: "*To-hic* has done no evil. I saw a white kid stung to death by a moccasin : I killed the snake. I was young then; now I am old, but my arm is not too withered to strike down the snake that stung To-hic. Where is the Iroquois?" There was a fierce, deathly gleam in the old pagan's eye as he looked around the circle of dusky faces who were watching him; they moved back, for as he moved his arm it lifted his blanket, and they saw that he wore a long, bright knife in his girdle, and a hatchet, keenly sharpened. But Ahdeek had long since slipped away, and was heard of, weeks afterwards, hunting in the forests of Maine. A grim look of contempt stole over Ma-kee's features, then he turned to Altontinon and said: "The snows of nearly eighty winters have brought me wisdom. I see what I see and know what I know. I found a young pigeon once in the forest, with its wing broken. I put it into a nest of young crows, and watched. The old mother crow came home and tore the pigeon to pieces to feed her own young." Then he marched off, well satisfied that he had struck no chance blow at Altontinon.

"It's no wonder old Ma-kee likes her," said Winonah, "since she goes to the Taho, and is a pagan like himself. But see! Coaina opens her eyes!" she cried, gazing down with gratified

malice on the mournful and beautiful face of her
cousin.

"Go for Father Etienne, Winonah. Friends,
stand back, and give the unfortunate one air and
water. She must not perish in her wickedness.
Oh, to think, after all my care—oh! oh! oh!"—
cried Altontinon, quite overcome, or rather pretending to be so.

Every one Winonah met on her way to Father
Etienne's, she told the news that Coaina had
"spent the night in the medicine lodge of the Iroquois, and assisted at their superstitious rites. She
went with Ahdeek, and everybody knew Ahdeek;
yes, she was at the Taho, and everybody knew
what *that* was."

"So," thought some, "we have been deceived."
But most of those who heard the strange and
dreadful news were shocked and bewildered. If
that bright and glorious star, worshipped with divine honors by their fathers in the primitive days,
and still regarded by the Indians as the most splendidly beauteous of all that spangle the blue robes
of heaven, had fallen a black and shapeless mass
at their feet, they could not have been more amazed
than at the fall of Coaina, in whom they had never
seen speck or flaw, and who was, after the Blessed

Virgin, the purest model of womanly and christian virtues they knew on earth. So blithe, so modest, so amiable towards all; "who," they wondered, "could ever feel envy or bitterness for Coaina? What enemies had she to plan such slanders? none. Then, alas! it must be true!" Alack-a-day! the evil days had indeed come for the young Algonquin maid, since even her best and dearest friends and kinsmen were deceived. There was none to help her on earth. Only the Great Spirit and His Immaculate Mother knew the innocence of that soul, which was to suffer such keen sorrows, holding it in a divine sanctuary; the powers of earth might crucify her flesh, but never pluck down or wither a single blossom of her crown; for *there* she was eternally safe. But having formed her life on theirs, she must drink, with resignation, of their bitter chalice—be, like Mary, suspected of evil, and, like Jesus, be reviled and cast out by her own people.

And the good Father Etienne—he was but human! There was no supernatural power to tell him that all this condemnatory, circumstantial evidence against Coaina was utterly false. He was speechless when Tar-ra-hee told him what he had witnessed with his own eyes. It seemed like the culminating proof of all else that had been whispered against her. When left alone, the good priest, with a sharp pang at heart, entered the sanctuary to mourn, in silence, over the fall of this child of many graces, who had not only given such scandal to religion, and humiliated christians, but had afforded a new triumph to the heathen and unbelievers, and to pray for guidance in conducting the trial on the morrow. Winonah waited long to see him, and when he, at length, left the chapel, she delivered her errand. Without speaking, he turned and walked quietly to Altontinon's lodge, which was, by this time, crowded with the friends and kinsmen of Altontinon and Tar-ra-hee, sitting or standing, in grave and boding silence, around the apartment, while in the midst, seated upon a rude bench, was Coaina, silent, pallid and drooping, her long, graceful hands folded together on her knees, while her attire, usually trim and neat, was damp and disarranged, and her long, rich tresses fell carelessly over her shoulders to the earthen floor. There she sat, like Job, accused of a hundred sins of which she was guiltless. There she sat, like her Lord in the hall of Pilate, awaiting the judgment of an extreme penalty for the crimes of others. Way was made for Father Etienne who, to the surprise of all, was followed by Tar-ra-hee, stern, grave and decorous, his rich blanket falling in graceful folds from his shoulders, and wearing no ornament except a large silver medal of the Blessed Virgin.

Coaina looked up when she saw the skirt of Father Etienne's *soutane*, with a gleam of hope in her eyes; but when she saw his stern countenance and averted eyes, and just behind him the grave and clouded face of Tar-ra-hee, over which gleamed not a single ray of pity, a vivid crimson dyed her face, neck and hands; her eyelids, heavy with their long, dusky lashes, drooped upon her cheeks, and her lips, now suddenly grown pallid, quivered with agony.

"Coaina," said Father Etienne, "stand up and speak the truth when I question you. For the sake of your own soul and religion, I adjure you, in the sacred names of Jesus and Mary, to speak the truth, and nothing but the truth."

"I will, my father," she answered, in a low, distinct tone, as she arose.

"Where did you spend the night?"

"In the medicine lodge of the Iroquois."

"What did you see there?"

"I saw the Taho."

"Were you taken to the medicine lodge by violence?"

"No, my father," she said, looking up with a bewildered expression.

"Who did you see there you knew?"

"Only Ahdeek, my father."

"Why did you go there, Coaina?"

"I got a letter from you telling me to come."

Here every dusky face leaned forward, and Father Etienne knitted his brows, while his face exhibited the strongest emotion.

"That is false, unfortunate child! It is also a slander," he said sternly. "Where is that letter?"

"I have it not, my father. Ahdeek tore it up."

"What did it say?" asked Father Etienne.

"It said, 'two girls of the Iroquois are dying, and will not be baptized until you come. Come quickly to the lodge beyond the pines outside the Iroquois village. That is what I remember. Your name, my father, was to it. I thought I obeyed you. After I got there I saw that I was entrapped, but I could not escape."

"That is a well got up story, Coaina; shame upon you!" said Altontinon, stepping forward. "No letter came to her, my father. Winonah says that none came. Winonah was sick, and I left Coaina to nurse her; but she left her and went away without saying where. It is like the mantle Ahdeek gave her. Ahdeek has been Coaina's lover since she was a child."

"Did Ahdeek give you that mantle, Coaina?" asked Father Etienne.

"I was told that—that—Tar-ra-hee had left it for me," she replied, gently.

"Oh, the bold one!" exclaimed her aunt. "I told her before Winonah that Ahdeek had brought her the mantle—she knows I did. And now 1 must speak. Coaina is not honest. She is not true. She steals my money, and sends it to Montreal to buy finery. She has told me many lies. My life has been worn out with her, and trying to hide her faults. Her ingratitude and hypocrisy I could bear, but I dared not let her carry dishonor into the lodge of Tar-ra-hee."

"There are calumnies," says a modern writer, "so great as to confuse innocence itself." Thus it was with poor Coaina. She saw that the evidence against her was strong, without being true. Events had encompassed her like a net, and confirmed all the slanders of her enemies. Everything made her appear more guilty; there was no witness to disprove the charges, and benumbed in her still anguish, she said not a word, but, "like a sheep before her shearers, she was dumb."

"Miserable child," said Father Etienne, breaking the breathless silence, while tears rolled unbidden over his aged cheeks. "There is nothing left for you but penance for your vices and crimes. You have brought great scandal on religion, you have wounded charity, you have been guilty of base ingratitude, you have outraged decency, and, to crown your sins, you have renewed the bitter Passion of Jesus Christ, and pierced with a sword of grief the heart of His tender Mother. I cannot pronounce your sentence until the assembly investigate your case and consult upon it. I came here hoping to find you innocent; I go away believing you guilty. Go to your room, and remain there until your people decide upon your punishment, and may Almighty God bring you to repentance."

Coaina arose, folded her hands upon her bosom, and bowed in token of obedience, then walked tremblingly away to the curtained corner of the lodge called hers. Lifting the curtain, she disappeared from the eyes of her traducers and enemies, and falling prostrate upon the floor, her soul sent up its strong appeal unto Him who alone knew her innocence; to Him who would never turn away from her, and on whose strong arm she could lean on this her day of tribulation; to Him in whom she would trust, even though He might slay her. But the passion of her grief was bitter. She was only human, and this casting of her out, this rending of the ties which had so long bound her to her friends, her director, her kinsmen, was terrible to bear, and gave separate and fierce wounds to her natural life, as each one was parted asunder. The cross was heavy to-day, but on the morrow it would become almost insupportable, while the clouds hanging gloomily above her would gather more darkly around her way.

CHAPTER VIII.

COAINA'S SENTENCE.

To DESCRIBE the judicial proceedings of the assembly in Coaina's case would stretch my narrative to a wearisome length; therefore, I will simply relate that, after due deliberation and a careful examination of the *apparent facts* of the case, those facts which, according to the judgment of all concerned, were incontestibly proved by credible witnesses, a verdict was rendered, and sentence pronounced on the beautiful and innocent Rose of the

Algonquins. Here I will quote from Monsigneur De C——'s statement.

Coaina was sentenced:

"*First.* To live alone in a hut adjoining her aunt's lodge.

"*Second.* To perform such servile offices for her as might be needed.

"*Third.* To seek and encourage no intercourse with the young people of the mission.

"*Fourth.* To wear the garb of a public penitent.

"*Fifth.* To have her hair cut close, and wear a coarse veil.

"*Sixth* (and the most terrible of all to her). She was to be deprived of the sacraments, and was forbidden to enter the chapel, but was to kneel in her penitential dress at the door, during the celebration of all the sacred rites, offices and ceremonies of the Church, with the title of *hypocrite* printed in large letters and suspended upon her breast."

On the same day she was invested in her robes of humiliation. Crowned with ignominy, she knelt at the door of that chapel of which she was the angel, receiving, instead of homage, the cold sneers, the cruel whispers, the open condemnation, the mockery and scorn of all who passed her by.

Let us pause here an instant, to discriminate

between the malice and hypocrisy of Coaina's enemies who *knew* her innocence, and the mistaken conviction of those of her former friends who believed her guilty. For the first there is no excuse; they deliberately and maliciously planned the desolation and ruin of that young life; they made it appear that a great and public scandal had been committed, and so perjured themselves as to deceive not only the good Father Etienne, but also the sincere christians of his flock, who thought her punishment, when measured by her apparent guilt, was not too heavy. The ill opinion of the wicked is without a sting; but when the good, the charitable and just, deceived by false reports, or otherwise, array themselves against one, then indeed an indescribale bitterness is added to the cup of woe, and the soul cries out, in the darkness and desolation of its abandonment: "My God! why hast Thou forsaken me?" All of Coaina's former friends and admirers could now only regard her as a hypocrite, who had long and speciously deceived them; so, full of horror at the reflection of her sacrilegious life, they shrunk from her as from a pestilence, and publicly resented the dishonor and scandal she had brought upon religion. And yet these were innocent before heaven, through the blindness of human judgment; the originators of the monstrous wrong were alone responsible for *all* the evil and *all* the scandal that had grown out of their selfish pride and malice. Old Ma-kee, who was a heathen, you know, caring neither for God or man, paid no heed to the *interdict*, and had no feeling except that of indignation at the humiliation of the only thing upon earth that he loved, and he resented it by disowning his people, as they had disowned her. It was he who gathered the wild forest flowers and brought them to her hut, or laid them beside her as she knelt at the chapel door; it was he whose harsh old quavering voice fell in accents of kindness upon her ear; he who, more than once, had given such sudden and well-aimed blows at the urchins who taunted and mocked her that they fell stunned and sprawling upon the grass. To Altontinon and Winonah he had become an incubus and terror. They cowered beneath the fierce gleam of the old pagan's eye, and would rather have heard the most deafening thunder that ever sped its bolt into the depths of the forest, than to hear old Ma-kee's bitter whisper of "Snakes! snakes! snakes!" hissed in their ear as they passed by.

Deeply touched by the old Indian's constant affection, Coaina prayed incessantly for his conversion, and also for that of her aunt and cousin, as well as of all others who had injured her. In fact, she, who had been cast out as unworthy by her people, was now their pleading angel, who forgot her wrongs in the exercise of a divine charity.

Father Etienne sorrowed and prayed for the poor penitent, who bore her cross with such sweetness and patience; he had at times a suspicion that she was the innocent victim of a base plot; but the mystery—if there was one—was too deep for him to fathom, and the scandal had been too public to go unpunished. And so the time passed until the next moon, when the Indians departed with their families and household effects, in their birchen canoes, for the distant northwest, where, surrounded by incredible hardships, they hunted the bison and the deer, the otter and the mink, the beaver and the bear, and other smaller game. Coaina accompanied them, still as a public penitent, and the servant of her aunt, the change bringing naught to her except greater hardships, which she bore without murmuring.

And so three years passed by. The mystery was still unsolved, and Coaina still wore her penitential garb, was still interdicted an approach to the sacraments, was still a by-word and reproach among her people. The only event of any importance in prospect, was the reported marriage of Tar-ra-hee and Winonah, for which it was said, preparations were being made. Ahdeek never reappeared among his people. It was rumored that in crossing the St. Lawrence in his canoe, it had been drawn into the whirl of the rapids, and dashed over the great falls into the foaming abyss below. An Indian certainly perished there about that time, within sight of thousands of spectators, and as he never returned or was heard of again, the inference was accepted that the unfortunate wretch was Ahdeek.

Again came the month of the falling leaves, and once more the mission was in a grand commotion, preparing for the annual migration to the distant hunting grounds, two thousand miles off. Father Etienne, as usual, was to accompany them. Another priest, a young and saintly missionary, who had fled from the endearments of noble kindred and home in his dear land of France; who had turned his back upon honors and all the charms of civilization, to labor among the heathen tribes of the far west—asked and gained permission to join company with them, an incident which was a great solace to Father Etienne, who was growing old. (Monsigneur De C.)

On a certain day they all embarked in their frail canoes, to start on their perilous voyage to the western plains. At certain places, to avoid the sweeping rapids, the terrific rocks and falls, they leave the river, carrying their canoes and baggage past the dangerous spots, when they again launch their frail vessels, and embark.

Bearing the same hardships and dangers as themselves, Father Etienne cheered and encouraged them as much by his counsel as his example, performing the offices of priest and comforter with tireless zeal, sometimes celebrating the holy mysteries on the bosom of some broad, calm river, with the picturesque fleet drawn up in perfect order around the floating altar, the paddles at rest, and gay pennons flying, while every dusky face and form in the gentle rocking canoes was bent with reverent and adoring attention towards the " canoe of prayer and sacrifice." These were occasions of deep and unutterable joy to our poor penitent, who, sometimes near, and sometimes farther off, in her aunt's canoe, witnessed the sacred mystery. Sometimes Mass was celebrated under the flame-colored branches of the primeval forest; sometimes on the mountain side; sometimes upon a desolate shore. But it was the great refreshment and consolation of this weary nomadic people, when and wherever celebrated. The place was nothing to them—the sacrament everything.

One sad incident occurred. The canoe in which the young French missionary, with four Abnaki Indians, were making the voyage, one day got far ahead of the mission flotilla, which proceeded slowly, on account of the dangerous rapids, whose current was powerfully felt long before they were seen; nor could all the signals which were made for them to return induce them to do so—probably they were misunderstood as cheering signals for them to proceed in the race they had won so far in advance. Suddenly the canoe was drawn into the mighty current, and whirled like a dead leaf amongst the foaming, shrieking waters; now lost to sight amid cataracts of spray, now tossed like a feather on the gale, high upon the surface, with five human beings clinging hopelessly to its sides, Then, in the twinkling of an eye, it was engulphed forever; the young missionary received the reward of eternal life for the mortal life he had so generously and nobly given to God's service.

At length, having arrived at the place best suited for their purposes, and most convenient for hunting, the Indians disembarked, and each family selecting a site, erected a wigwam of boughs, which they covered with skins sewed together. In a short time the business of the winter begins; the men, and women also, hunt and fish continually, living upon the animals they kill; dressing the skins, and preserving with great care the costly furs, which they sell readily in Montreal for high prices, and to traders from the United States. In this hunting expedition no one was more expert or successful than Coaina in securing much costly game. Her aim was unerring, and when she drew the string of her bow her arrow sped like lightning into a vital part of the animal, without tearing the fur. Swans, wild turkeys, an eagle, and small game of every kind, loaded her aunt's wigwam, who, with Winonah, prepared the peltry for the markets, sheltered from cold, and enduring no real hardships. But still they found no kind word for the patient Coaina. Injurious epithets, blows, scanty fare, and hardships of every kind were her reward. What incited them to greater malignity, was the fact that Tar-ra-hee had left his people, at the mouth of the Sauganay, to spend the winter with some of his braves on its bleak shores, to hunt the white bear, the seal and the beaver, and for this disappointment they wreaked their spite on Coaina, whose heart, sore, and almost breaking under the torture of her undeserved ill-usage, clung tremblingly and closer to Jesus and Mary, fearful that after all she should lose patience and forfeit her only good. But nothing touched the hearts of these evil-minded, obdurate women; her very patience and defencelessness, so far from appealing to their generosity and forbearance, seemed to excite them to greater cruelty and malice. No one observed it, but Coaina's cheek had lost its beautiful roundness of outline; her step, still swift and agile, was often checked by shortness of breath, and wild, painful heart-throbs. The rich blood no longer glowed in transparent suffusion through her amber-colored skin, and delicately chiseled lips; there was a spot of crimson upon each thin cheek, like the first reddening flame which consumes the life of the maple leaf in autumn. Her eyes—now seldom lifted—sparkled with a strange glow beneath her heavy eye-lids, and when suddenly raised by some one speaking to her, or in surprise at some distant sound, they looked like those of a hunted gazelle. Outcast and despised, her communings had long ceased to be of this life, or of its small affairs. The world had thrown her off as more worthless than the refuse of a dung-hill; but could the veil have been, but one moment, withdrawn, could mortal eyes have, but for one instant, beheld the "glorious ones in shining raiment" who surrounded her, who enfolded her within the embraces of their stainless wings, guarding her soul's integrity as a precious and priceless jewel, they would have fallen upon their faces before her, invoking her forgiveness and prayers.

But neither to her or them was such sight vouchsafed. The designs of God must ripen according to His wisdom, and for Coaina the consummation was near at hand.

CHAPTER IX.

THE TWO SHADOWS.

THE season of leaves and flowers had again rolled round; the bluebird whistled in the air, and the bobolink sounded his low bugle as he raided with his brown troopers through the feathery ferns. Everything wore a gay and prosperous look in the village of the lake. The hunting season had been extremely successful, not only in the quantity of game secured, but in the quality and abundance of rare furs, skins, and other valuable peltries they were enabled to bring home. Better still, the price of peltries had gone up considerably higher than was ever known before, owing to an increased demand from the United States and England, which was really in excess of the supply; hence our Indians of the mission found themselves richer than they had ever been before. On Sundays and holidays the church looked like a tropical *parterre*, with the array of rich, bright colors in the attire of the women, whose new variegated handkerchiefs, blue scarfs, scarlet petticoats, spangled jackets and fringed tunics, were in harmonious keeping with the magnificent hunting shirts—decorated with beads and fringes—of the men, who displayed new scarlet leggings, wrought curiously with porcupine quills, and moccasins flaming with scarlet, with glittering beads and tinsel. Altontinon and Winonah held their heads higher than ever, while the extreme gaudiness of their apparel, extravagant both in texture and style, attracted every eye. While the other women and young girls observed a fitting degree of moderation and modesty in their attire, these two flaunted about arrayed in the gaudiest colors, the flashiest trinkets, the heaviest coils of beads, and the most exaggerated style of garments that the wildest Indian fancy could suggest, or the markets of Montreal supply.

A great improvement was also evident in the increased comforts of their rude lodges, in the richer adornment of their beloved chapel, and the quality and quantity of their agricultural implements; indeed, the village of the "Lake of the Two Mountains" seemed like the centre of a happy pastoral Arcadia, into which no grief could enter.

In the midst of all this gay prosperity and cheerful plenty, there was ever moving to and fro, or kneeling with bowed head at the chapel door, a silent, shadowy form, clothed in coarse, penitential garments of grey. This shadowy, veiled figure was never noticed, except to be jostled aside and scoffed at as it glided through the mission grounds. And it moved like one walking in a dream. If she was jostled rudely, or called out to roughly, or had her veil or garments plucked at by the village urchins, she would suddenly lift her great soft eyes, and with a bright, wild glance around, as if she had been startled from solemn reverie, deep within her inner life, smile sorrowfully, look down again, and move on.

There was this shadow, which the Algonquins saw daily; a shadow for whose presence they had only contempt, or a silent indifference—the shadow of a crushed life, the summing up of all that slander could do.

But there was another shadow coming towards them, slowly and inevitably, the very thought of which made the bravest heart among them quail. This shadow had already reached Montreal, and they even now felt the vibrations of its noiseless but mighty tread, already felt the cold thrill of its viewless form. They could not keep it away; neither barriers nor all the engineering that science has ever taught—neither the bravery of warriors, the exorcism of priests, nor the tears and prayers of a people, could stay its course, because it was the stern messenger of the Most High, whose mission it was to chasten, to punish and remind the world of the judgment to come. It was the *cholera!* and as it strode towards them, while every face wore an anxious, a sad or thoughtful expression, the face of the other shadow which was clothed in the robes of penance grew more serene and bright, as if that which brought such terror to all, only came a messenger of hope to her. And so it was. "If it were only the Great Spirit's sweet will," she thought, "it will bring one deliverance and rest; but His will, not mine, be done!"

One day—it was a bright and glorious morning, just such a one as that on which the malignant plans laid for Coaina's ruin seemed crowned with success—there suddenly arose from Altontinon's lodge, shrill, piercing cries of pain, blended with the mournful *wakonowin*. The shadow had come! it had entered Altontinon's lodge, and stricken her down even while she exulted in her health, her wickedness and her prosperity. Messengers ran here and there for assistance. Father Etienne was soon beside her writhing, tortured form, but her kinsmen and people stood aloof, cowering outside the lodge, their hearts quailing within them as her shrieks of agony rent the air. While she wrestled for life with this awful shadow, the shadow in the garments of penance ministered to her needs. It was Coaina (obeying the directions of Father Etienne) who applied the hot poultices, who administered the fiery draughts which were thought efficacious, and which *were* marvellously so in ordinary cases; it was she who performed the most repulsive offices for the agonized woman, who wept over her, who clung to her cramped hands, who kissed her cold feet, and prayed without ceasing for her. None else would come near or touch her. Winonah, trembling and pallid, crouched in a distant corner, her head bowed upon her knees, incapable of performing the slightest duty. Suddenly Altontinon cried out: "I wronged her! I ruined her! She is innocent of all! Coaina, forgive me! forgive me! You are an angel! I am a devil! O, pray for me to the Holy Mother! Do not let me be cast into hell! O, save me from the flames! Hold me fast, Coaina! O, Christ, forgive me! Coaina, *forgive* me!"

"I forgive thee, my aunt, as I hope Christ will forgive me," she answered, kissing the blue, trembling lips of the dying sinner.

"Father Etienne, hear me! hear me! I will confess——" but here ensued such a mortal struggle that she was unable to continue. Her head was drawn round, her features, pinched and blue, were distorted with agony, and her arms and legs, drawn away, were knotted in muscular distortions fearful to behold. Father Etienne, startled by her confession of guilt, feared that the last agony was upon her, and knelt to pray for her departing soul. Coaina, also praying, bathed her feet with her tears. But the paroxysm subsided, and an interval of comparative ease ensued—of ease which was but the forerunner of that rest from suffering which the tortured body would soon enjoy.

"Call my child—call my kindred around me," said Altontinon, in feeble tones. "Quick, tell them to come, I have many words to say before them."

Father Etienne said: "Your confession first; your confession; then, what time you have left, say all that you wish."

"It is my confession. I must confess in public the evil I did in secret. O, my father, call them quickly, or I die!" plead Altontinon.

Father Etienne did as she desired, but it was only by the most urgent entreaties that he could get Winonah and the rest to approach the dying woman, whose shrunken features and pallid skin, which already hung loose and wrinkled from her bones, were dripping with the cold dews of dissolution, while the blue, ghastly shadow threw its cadaverous hue over it all. The group of her kinsmen and friends who entered stood some distance off, looking with dread at her changed appearance.

"Now," she said, "listen to my words, for this is my last confession. I ruined *her* by my malice," she continued, pointing her shrunken and almost powerless hand to Coaina; "because I wanted my own child to be the wife of Tar-ra-hee. I held counsel with Ahdeek, the Iroquois, who brought the robe, and I made up the story that Tar-ra-hee had left it for Coaina, and wished her to wear it to meet him on the shore. *I* wrote the letter that beguiled her to the medicine lodge! I set Tar-ra-hee to watch her! I arranged the whole plot to expose her! I persuaded my kinsmen to circulate evil reports about her! I made my own child lie, and make oath to her lie, that Coaina was a thief! *I did it!* Coaina is guiltless! No baptized babe could be purer! O, Coaina! can you forgive me!"

"My child," said Father Etienne, tears flowing over his cheeks, as he approached and knelt before Coaina, "my child, can you forgive us all?"

"O, my father!" cried Coaina, covered with confusion, as she knelt, and lifting the hem of his *soutane*, pressed it to her lips, "this is too much."

"Say, my child, that you forgive us," said Father Etienne.

"O, my father! yes, yes! ten thousand, thousand times—but no! what have I to forgive? O, my aunt! if you knew the peace and consolation that sufferings have brought me, you would rejoice, and be glad!" exclaimed Coaina, while her countenance shone with a divine peace. There was no exultation to mar its serenity, or cloud the tender pity of her eyes, now resting upon the face of Altontinon.

"O, my father, darkness gathers around me," said Altontinon, in a low, solemn voice. "Coaina, do you forgive me?"

"As I hope Christ to forgive me, so do I forgive you with all my heart and soul," she replied.

"Then will *He* forgive me! Oh, my sins! my sins! Father, help me! The shadows grow darker—the winds colder," cried Altontinon, shuddering.

Father Etienne made a sign, and all withdrew from the presence of the fast sinking woman—her guilty accomplices filled with confusion and dread; the others bewildered by the strange revelations and appalling scenes they had witnessed; all withdrew except Coaina, whose hand was held fast in the death grasp of Altontinon. Father Etienne leaned over and heard her low murmuring words of penitence; her voice was almost gone, or she would have declared her sins aloud; in view of her great guilt, and the near approach of the dread judgment, no motive of human respect or shame could have withheld her; her only desire *now* was to relieve her conscience, that she might depart in the humble hope of one day finding safety and peace. Convinced of her true penitence, Father Etienne administered Extreme Unction, and pronounced the last absolution. She was too far gone to receive the supreme and crowning consolation of the Holy Viaticum.

"Does Coaina forgive me?" she whispered again.

"Coaina's prayers have obtained your conversion; doubt not, then, her forgiveness in this extreme hour," said Father Etienne.

"Have you prayed for me, Coaina? Through it all, Coaina? Can it be? Tell me, child!" she moaned.

"I have never ceased praying for you, my aunt," she replied, as she stooped down and kissed Altontinon's damp forehead, already marbled by the touch of death.

Then, for the first time, tears flowed from Altontinon's darkened eyes, and she whispered, almost gasping: "Call upon the holy names that I dare not speak; and while Father Etienne read the office for the dying, Coaina whispered over and over again in her ear the names of JESUS and MARY. She lay so silent and motionless they thought her dead, when she suddenly cried out: "Jesus, forgive," striking her breast with her shriveled hand; and with these words upon her lips, with her hand uplifted to inflict another self-accusing blow, the troubled soul of Altontinon passed away to the tribunal of Infinite Justice, where, we trust—despite her sins and misdeeds—it found safe shelter in the infinite mercy of Him who pardoned the dying thief.

Ere night settled upon the panic-stricken village, Winonah lay dead beside her mother. Confessing her sins, she humbly asked pardon of Coaina, whom she had so cruelly assisted to injure, and, above all, for the public scandal produced by her malice and falsehoods, and died a few hours after she was stricken by the pestilence, in great agony and deep perturbation of soul.

Coaina had "missed the crown, but not the stake of martyrdom." The penitent confessions of Altontinon and Winonah, before so many witnesses, removed the stigma from her name and reputation. All were as anxious now to obtain a look or word from her as they were before eager to avoid her.

By what most people would call a remarkable coincidence, but which Monsigneur De C——, who was deeply versed in the ways of God, styled retributive justice, the first victims of cholera in that Algonquin village were Altontinon, Winonah, and five of their kinsfolk who were leagued with them in the wicked plot against the innocent Coaina, who perished, one after another, publicly confessing his or her agency in the affair, while they made the most solemn asseverations of her perfect innocence.

Like an angel, Coaina walked unscathed amidst the pestilence ; her grey, penitential garments, so lately the insignia of her disgrace, were now honored as no royal robes were ever honored, and hailed with blessings afar and near; wherever she appeared, those who had slandered, defamed and made a mock of her, would fain have knelt and kissed the frayed and faded serge, had she allowed it. But such homage could not move her soul from its strong entrenchments upon that rock whither the storms of obloquy and humiliation had driven her, and where, in divine crucibles, the dross of her nature had been separated from the precious gold. With sweet and gentle words she received their repentant expressions of kindness, but hastened away from all who sought to detain her, to minister to the sick and dying. Standing or kneeling beside them, assisting Father Etienne in all that she could, holding the poor hands stiffening in death, or smoothing the cold forehead knotted with agony; reciting the prayers and aspirations which their feeble tongues could no longer utter; performing the most menial offices, shrinking, in fact, from nothing that she could do for the dying or convalescent, she gave herself but scant rest day or night until the dread pestilence, leaving behind its broad furrows of graves, passed away from among them, through the forests, southward.

CHAPTER X.

CROWNING.

It was with great joy that Coaina once more approached the divine sacraments. Like a pilgrim long abroad, and lost in a dreary wilderness, who suddenly finds himself at home, surrounded by its peaceful and holy endearments, and partaking of its joyful feasts, as one perishing with thirst in an arid desert suddenly beholds a cool fountain gush from the burning sands beside him; so felt she while kneeling at the shrine of our Blessed Lady, or before the altar to receive the Bread of refreshment and eternal life. Every moment, not devoted to the sick and to necessary repose, she spent in the chapel; it was her home, her refuge, her palace; it was to her the vestibule of heaven and the shadow of its everlasting repose, where she sat undisturbed at the feet of Jesus and Mary.

Old Ma-kee crept here and there after her, watching and waiting patiently her coming and going, seemingly satisfied if he could keep her in sight, for he seldom spoke. Towards the people of the mission, he preserved the most dignified *hauteur*, only condescending to speak to them when he had an opportunity to say something very bitter; in fact old Ma-kee was a sort of moral nettle, stinging right and left, which helped the rash-minded in their penance, and gave the more humble something to think about. He was only an old pagan, we know, and it was his way to judge of a tree by its fruits; he was one of those witnesses no one thinks about, who will arise in the latter day to testify for or against the fidelity of christians to their opportunities and graces.

It was Sunday morning, and the mission chapel was crowded with those whom the pestilence had spared. Father Etienne had appointed that day not only as one of solemn thanksgiving, but was determined, with all the beautiful chivalry of his nation, and the still more noble chivalry of christianity, to make use of the opportunity to offer a public *amende* to Coaina, whose great humiliations had not only been public, but so entirely unmerited.

She, all unaware of what was coming, knelt in her old accustomed place, partly sheltered from view by a cluster of cedar posts. After Father Etienne had spoken in the most simple but impressive manner, and with touching pathos, of the great mercy of God in having spared them while the pestilence was abroad, and told them how in gratitude they were more than ever bound to love and honor their Heavenly Protectress, of whom they were the special care, and devote themselves to Almighty God and His service by a stricter obedience to the rules of faith, and a closer observance of the requirements of charity; then he proposed that all should unite with him in saying the decade of the five Dolorous Mysteries of the Rosary, for the repose of the souls of those who had recently fallen victims to the scourge of the pestilence. Instantly, every knee was devoutly bent, and every head bowed, while the soul-touching devotion, with its solemn prayers and responses, was performed. Low sobs and fast falling tears attested the deep emotion felt by the congregation, and there is no doubt that the earnest and pathetic appeal to the mercy-seat in behalf of those who could no longer help themselves amidst the sweet torture of flame and exile, fell like refreshing dews upon their patient and suffering souls.

This over, the good priest then spoke of Coiana, who shrunk out of sight when she heard her name, covered with confusion and humility. He related, in brief and simple language, the great wrongs that had been inflicted upon her, then declared how utterly groundless had been even the slightest suspicion of her; how guiltless she had been of the least crime charged against her; how each one who had slandered and conspired against her, had separately acknowledged their crime, and asserted her innocence with their dying breath; and then, turning toward where she knelt hidden by the cedar pillars and closely veiled, he asked in the name of all present, her forgiveness. Then he spoke to these simple children of the forest of the error of rash judgment, of the damnable sin of slander, of the bitter evils of envy, of the malice of pride, of the blighting effects of uncharitableness, which opens the door of the soul to all of the capital sins; after which he concluded by contrasting with these, the beauty of humility, the virtue of silence, the eternal fruits of penitence, the holiness of patience, the glory of true charity, and the divine virtue of forgiveness. All understood it. Not one there who would not have kissed the hem of Coaina's garment; but what was their astonishment when— as Coiana with bowed head and meekly folded hands, approached the altar and knelt to receive the "food of Angels"—they saw old Ma-kee, who had been crouching somewhere out of sight, creep slowly forward, stand a moment erect and then kneel at Father Etienne's feet beside her, asking for baptism! It was from no want of knowledge, but of faith, that he had deferred and put aside christianity so long—he knew all that it taught; he had been living too long among christians, and was too shrewdly intelligent, and intelligently curious to be ignorant of christian doctrine or dogma, and now by some wonderful operation of Divine Providence—possibly in answer to Coaina's prayers, and to reward his charity toward her during the days of her tribulation—here at the last moment, just when the last sands were crumbling away from his frail foothold on life; the grace of faith was once more proffered him, not to be rejected again. That afternoon at vespers Ma-kee received the regenerating waters of baptism, putting off his old savage cognomen, won more than half a century before by his dexterity in scalping the victims which fell beneath his war club in the last fierce wars of his tribe, and received in its stead that of Peter. Ma-kee's conversion made quite a festival at the mission of the Two Mountains, but after it was over, the old chief was seen no more among them. He lay down one night upon his couch of skins, where he lingered month after month, suffering from an incurable disease. He was removed on a litter to Coaina's lodge, where she nursed him with all the fidelity and tenderness of a daughter. Father Etienne saw him daily and comforted him with good counsel and cheering words. Except to these two he had but few words to say. When his friends, kinsmen and others of his tribe, young and old, flocked to see him, he had but one admonition, which he gave individually to them all, and repeated again whenever they came; this was: "JUDGE NOT." Unlike the beloved disciple at Patmos, he did not say: "Little children love one another;" Ma-kee was of sterner stuff, and had he been in the vigor of his prime, he would have been just as apt as not, had occasion offered, to have *enforced* his admonition by smiting off offenders' ears and otherwise inflicting such just punishment as the case in hand required. But he was too far gone now to do aught—to keep them in mind of the great sin of rash judgment and uncharitableness they had fallen into against his favorite—except say to them, one and all, "*Judge not*," and they remembered the solemn sentence, after the old chief was laid in his christian grave until the end of their days.

All was changed for Coaina, but she remained

unchanged, except that her soul ripened in virtue and grace. She would fain have continued to wear her grey robes of penance, but Father Etienne represented to her that they were a daily reproach to every one in the village, reminding them of their injustice against her, and expressed his own desire that she should leave them off; then for the sake of charity, and in a spirit of obedience, she did so, and wore a dress and veil of fine cloth, embroidered and faced with white silk, which the ladies of Montreal, who had heard her strange story, had sent to Father Etienne for her acceptance.

Tar-ra-hee, who had been faithful to her in heart, again sought her for his wife, and other alliances equally as honorable were offered, but she rejected them all with modest and gentle dignity, saying: "I have found my true and constant Lover, He not only comforted and sustained me, when all else failed, and the world abandoned me; but He also suffered and died for me."

Ah, happy she to have so early tested the nothingness of this life, and tasted so soon the bitter lees of its flower-crowned cup; most happy for her, that the staff upon which she had leaned in thoughtless security, broke in twain, piercing her and driving her to the support of one which would support her in the "valley of the shadow of death." For Coaina was fading away from this life; her eyes grew brighter, and her cheeks wore that crimson hue, which harbingers dissolution, as the reddening of the forest leaves tells of the death fires which consume their life. Her step, once so swift and light, became feeble and slow; and ere long, she was confined to her lodge. *"Changed from penitential silence to a place of pilgrimage, her abode became the resort of people from far and near. As they go to visit the relics and shrines of saints, they came to look upon her; to hear a last word from her lips, to inhale the odor of her virtues, and recommend themselves to her prayers. I saw one, who went in to visit her, come hastily out —the big tears rolling over his face—saying: 'I am unworthy to remain longer in the presence of such an angel.'"

Fading away like the morning star into the brightness of dawn, Coaina—all unmoved except to deeper humility by all the prodigal attentions lavished upon her, and scarcely understanding the interest she excited, so unconscious was she of any superior excellence—felt that her end was drawing near. It was past midnight, and so far from any

* Monseigneur De C——.

appearance of approaching dissolution about her, her friends who had been watching beside her, thought they had not seen her look so well and strong for many weeks. There was a look of joy in her face, an elasticity in her motions, and a clear musical ring in her voice which filled them with astonishment, and hope that she was yet to be spared to them. But it was only the girding-up of the pilgrim, who, after his toilsome march, sees through the mist the joyful glimmer upon the walls of the city, where his weary form will find rest and his toils their crown and reward. She was dying, dying in cheerful hope, and calmly made her preparations for the event. She asked for her richest garments, those which she had fashioned with such taste and care nearly four years ago, for her wedding attire, composed of rich stuffs of various and beautiful colors, adorned with brilliant feathers, with pearls and silver and gold fringes; and with the assistance of her friends, arrayed herself in it. Bathing her face and hands, she smoothed back her beautiful hair, now grown long and silky, and placed upon her head the exquisite wreath of feather flowers and pearls, sent to her by the nuns of Notre Dame; she composed herself upon her pillow, her hands folded upon her bosom, holding her beloved rosary, which she continued to recite, while she awaited with serene composure the coming of Father Etienne (who had been sent for) with the Holy Viaticum. Soon he came and gave her the holy anointing, all present uniting fervently in the prayers, while they watched through their tears the kindling brightness of her face; after which he approached her, holding in his veiled hands the Most Holy Viaticum, the Bread which consoleth, the Lamb which taketh away all sin. She stretched out her thin dusky hands toward the Divine Guest, and while her eyes glowed with unearthly lustre, she exclaimed in clear, sweet tones: "Welcome, beloved Lord. I bless Thee, my God, that I have been counted worthy to be treated some little like Thy Divine Son; and I bless and forgive, ten thousand times, all who ever injured me. Come, sweet Jesus, it is now that my wedding feasts are about to begin, never to end!"

These were the last words uttered by Coaina, for after having received the Holy Viaticum, and last absolution, she lay with folded hands, her large bright eyes fixed upon the crucifix and the image of Mary at the foot of her bed, speechless and motionless, and they thought, as they gazed upon her with tender awe, that she held communication with angels, all unseen by them. Beautiful—by the flickering light of tapers, which glistened with fitful rays among the gold and silver trimmings of her bridal dress, flashing out here and there, as with hidden glories—looked the Indian maiden; but more fair and lovely looked she, when the first golden sunbeams stole through the vines, and lighted up those soft tender eyes, now gazing upon far greater and more distant glories—for she was dead. No one knew the moment of her passing away, it was so serene. Her tender and faithful devotion to the Immaculate Mother of Jesus, her patient virtues so like unto hers, crowned this supreme hour with peace, and obtained for her, we trust, swift admission to the ineffable joys of her Divine Son.

Certain it is, that the remembrance of the gentle Coaina's devotion to the Blessed Mother—under whose invocation the Mission was established over a century before—combined with a knowledge of the fruits thereof, which they had all witnessed, not only in the conversion of her enemies, but the increased ardor of the people of the Mission, added but another link to the glittering chain of evidence which stretches from the humble house of Nazareth, through the hoary centuries, down to our own times, of the efficacy of the powerful intercession of the Virgin Mother, whose Immaculate Conception cannot be doubted without doubting God; for if He, by His Divine power, created Eve, who was to become the mother of men, pure and spotless, who will dare doubt that by the same Divine power, suspending the common laws of fallen nature, He created pure and without blemish, her, who from all eternity was predestined to the wonderful dignity of becoming the Mother of His Divine Son. Of her flesh was formed His; who then can believe that that virginal flesh had taint or stain of the pollution of the fall? Let us hail thee, then, our Immaculate Mother and tender friend, given to us by Almighty God from His high throne in heaven; bequeathed to us by Jesus from the bloody Cross on Calvary! hail thee as our compassionate intercessor with thy Son, who is to be our Judge, imploring thee, who partook of all the bitterness of the cup He drained for our salvation, and who knowest so well our human infirmities, to obtain for us such graces that these august sufferings and infinite ransom may not, through our own fault, become useless to us.

We have concluded the narrative of Coaina, the Rose of the Algonquins, and will close by once more quoting from Monseigneur De C——: "Her burial was more like a triumph than a scene of mourning, and to this day she is honored and invoked by the christians of the mission of the 'Lake of the Two Mountains,' as virgin, and martyr to false testimony.

[The following is the autograph to which we have alluded in the commencement of COAINA. It was written by Monsigneur de Charbonnel, Bishop of Toronto, C. W., when he was studying the English language at Saint Mary's Seminary, Baltimore. Subsequently, having received permission from the Holy Father, he resigned the mitre, and retired to a cloister of one of the contemplative Orders in Europe:]

We have near Montreal a Catholic congregation of Indian savages. Their village is situated on the banks of a beautiful lake formed by the waters of the Ottawa, and crowned with two very pleasant little mountains. Hence this village is called the Lake of the Two Mountains.

There was in this village a young Indian girl, still living last year; I will call her Coaina (Catherine). She was an orphan, educated by her aunt.

Almighty God, the special Father of orphans, granted this girl so many graces, and she was so faithful to His inspirations, that, so striking was her piety, docility, modesty and amiability, she possessed the esteem and affection of all the village. She made the family of her aunt happy, and parents proposed her to their children as a model to imitate. From her first years, like those of her tribe, she was employed in hunting.

Every autumn they leave their village, and start with all their little children to the northwest. Every family embarks in its small and very light canoe, and with this frail vessel goes up the river and lakes two thousand miles distant. In certain places they leave the river, on account of the dreadful rapids through the rocks and falls, and carry their canoes and baggage around. Their happiness is to have with them a missionary, to follow them during all their hunting. It is not two years since that one priest was drowned, with all those who were in the same canoe. Glorious and happy death for a priest devoted to the glory of God and good of souls! Arrived at the woods, in places excellent for hunting, every family erects a hut with trees and branches to pass the winter. All their occupation during that season is to hunt;

they live on the animals which they kill or catch, and at their return they sell the skins of these animals, whose furs are so well appreciated in our cities as a defence against the sharpness of the winter. You may judge how hard must be such a life through rivers and lakes and woods, rain and snow, frost and ice, particularly for the tender children.

However, our young girl, in this manner of living, became as strong, as skilful a huntress, as she was pious and amiable. No one surpassed her in running, in jumping, in climbing up the trees, in shooting; but she surpassed all the others in piety and modesty. Accomplished as Coaina was, the son of the chief of the tribe wished to marry her, and the marriage was to be soon celebrated with great feasts through the village, when all was stopped and changed. Her aunt charged her with many crimes; the judges of the tribe held their solemn assembly to decide the case; witnesses were heard, and on their depositions the accused girl was convicted of several crimes, and condemned to a public penance, and as much despised as she was before esteemed and praised by everybody. For several years the coming in the church and the receiving of the holy Communion were forbidden to her; during the offices, when people were coming in or going out, she was obliged to kneel down or stand outside of the door of the temple, with a dress of penance, and the title of a hypocrite.

Meanwhile the cholera broke out; all the relatives of Coaina were seized, and her aunt the first, and more severely than the others. In fear of death, judgment and hell, she called the priest and the judges, and declared that all the accusations against her neice were but lies, false testimony, calumnies inspired by the devil of jealousy, because her neice had been preferred to her own daughter by the son of the chief of the tribe; all the other accusers confessed the same before they died Hence, our innocent victim was not now esteemed, as before her condemnation, like a saint, but an angel. The most advantageous alliances were proposed to her, but she refused them all, to belong more closely to God alone.

The year before last, Coaina was taken sick; during her sickness her cottage was changed into a place of pilgrimage—every one came to her, as people go to the relics of the saints, wishing to see her again, to hear a last word from her mouth, to inhale the odor of her virtues, to recommend themselves to her prayers; and one day a public sinner being invited to visit the holy sick—I, said he, shedding some big tears, I, to approach such an angel! I am unworthy of it.

Coaina, feeling death very near, asked for her full dress, composed of stuffs of various and brilliant colors, adorned with feathers, pearls, silver and gold fringes, received the sacraments with the most edifying fervor, blessing God for having been treated a little as her innocent Saviour, and forgiving a thousand times her calumniators. Her confessor, who would not speak when she was condemned, said now that her aunt and relations were indebted for their conversion to the fervent prayers which she did not cease to say in their behalf during her penance. What a heroical charity!

Her last words were these: It is now that my wedding feasts are going to begin, not to end. Her burial was rather a triumph than a mourning. Everybody in the village honors and invokes her as a virgin, and a martyr of false testimonies.

God tries sometimes, but never gives up the just; and He always rewards them, here and in heaven, according to their generosity in trials and crosses. Pray for your servant in Christ,

A. CHARBONNEL.

P. O'SHEA'S
New Publications,
AND
NEW EDITIONS OF IMPORTANT BOOKS.

LACORDAIRE'S WORKS.

LACORDAIRE'S CONFERENCES ON GOD.
One vol. royal 8vo, cloth, bevelled........................$3.00

LACORDAIRE'S CONFERENCES ON OUR LORD JESUS CHRIST.
One vol. royal 8vo, cloth................................$3.00

LACORDAIRE'S CONFERENCES ON THE CHURCH.
One vol. royal 8vo......................................$5.00

LIVES OF THE DECEASED BISHOPS OF THE CATHOLIC CHURCH IN THE UNITED STATES.
By RICHARD H. CLARKE, A.M. Two vols. imperial 8vo, superbly printed, bound, and illustrated........................$8.00

GENERAL HISTORY OF THE CHURCH.
By DARRAS. With an Introduction and Notes by Archbishop Spalding. Four vols. 8vo, cloth........................$12.00

SERMONS FOR THE TIMES.
By Rev. D. A. MERRICK, S.J. One vol. 12mo, elegantly printed and bound..$1.50

LECTURES ON THE CHURCH.
By Rev. D. A. MERRICK, S.J. One vol. 12mo............$1.50

RULES FOR THE CHOICE OF A STATE OF LIFE.
By Rev. R. F. AUG. DAMANET. S.J. Cloth................ 80

MANUAL OF THE HOLY NAME OF JESUS.
An elegant Prayer-Book, specially recommended to young men. By the DOMINICAN FATHERS. Flexible morocco.............. $1.00

THE AGNUS DEI: ITS HISTORY AND USE.
By a Father of the Society of Jesus. Flexible cloth.... 20

THE CROWN OF MARY; OR, THE ROSARY.
With Illustrations and Meditations. By a DOMINICAN FATHER. 18mo, paper.. 10

THE KNOWLEDGE AND LOVE OF JESUS CHRIST.
By Rev. FATHER SAINT JURE, S.J. Three vols., cloth, bevelled... $7.50

THE SPIRIT OF SAINT FRANCIS OF SALES.
One vol. 12mo, cloth, bevelled.......................... $2.00

MEDITATIONS FOR EVERY DAY IN THE YEAR.
By Rev. FATHER CRASSET, S.J........................... $1.80

TREATISE ON THE LOVE OF GOD.
By SAINT FRANCIS DE SALES. One vol. 12mo............. $1.75

INTRODUCTION TO A DEVOUT LIFE.
By SAINT FRANCIS OF SALES. 18mo...................... 75

INSTRUCTIONS ON THE COMMANDMENTS AND SACRAMENTS.
By St. LIGUORI. 32mo................................... 40

THE CATHOLIC YOUTH'S HYMN-BOOK.
The best collection of Catholic Hymns extant, with music, &c., &c. Compiled by the BROTHERS OF THE CHRISTIAN SCHOOLS, with a special view to the WANTS of CATHOLIC SCHOOLS. 4to...... 60
———— Cheap edition, *without music*................... 15

THE ILLUSTRATED PROGRESSIVE SERIES OF READING AND SPELLING BOOKS.
THE BEST SERIES PUBLISHED.

P. O'SHEA, Publisher
27 Barclay Street, New York

www.ingramcontent.com/pod-product-compliance
Lightning Source LLC
Chambersburg PA
CBHW030351170426
43202CB00010B/1331